AIR FRYER COOKBOOK
for Beginners

From breakfast to dessert: How to prepare healthy, quick and delicious dishes with the Airfryer, all illustrated with beautiful color photos.

Magda Jones

Table of Contents

Chapter 1: Introduction to the Air Fryer

What is an air fryer?

The hot air fryer is an innovative kitchen appliance that has become very popular in recent years. It allows us to prepare delicious and crunchy dishes without having to give up a low-fat diet.

But what exactly is an air fryer? Basically, it is a device that works using hot air and a fan. Instead of oil or fat, as is the case with conventional deep fryers, the food in the hot air fryer is cooked using hot air. This means the food is cooked gently and evenly, leaving it crispy on the outside and tender on the inside.

The hot air fryer offers numerous advantages over conventional deep fryers. For one thing, it only requires a fraction of the amount of oil or fat, which contributes to a healthier diet. At the same time, you also save yourself the hassle of disposal and the odor problem that can arise when deep-frying.

Another great advantage of the air fryer is its versatility. It is not only suitable for deep-frying, but also for grilling, baking and roasting. In addition to French fries and chicken nuggets, you can also prepare healthy vegetable chips, crispy chicken wings or delicious mini pizzas.

In my book "The XXL Hot Air Fryer Recipe Book" you will find many healthy and delicious recipes for beginners and professionals, all with tips and tricks. From hearty main courses to light snacks and tempting desserts - the hot air fryer offers endless possibilities for creative cooking.

Immerse yourself in the world of the hot air fryer and discover new taste experiences without regrets. Be inspired by the diverse recipes and surprise your loved ones with healthy and delicious dishes that can be prepared in no time. The simple hot air fryer recipe book XXL is the perfect companion for anyone who wants to get the most out of their hot air fryer.

Benefits of Using an Air Fryer

In today's chapter, we will look at the numerous benefits of using an air fryer. Whether you are a beginner or a professional in the kitchen, this innovative kitchen appliance will surely revolutionize your cooking experiences.

One of the main advantages of an air fryer is its healthy cooking method. Unlike traditional deep fryers, it requires a minimal amount of oil to prepare crispy and delicious dishes. This allows you to enjoy low-fat meals without sacrificing taste. For those who want to keep an eye on their diet, the air fryer is the perfect choice.

Another big advantage is the time saving. The air fryer heats up quickly and allows you to prepare your dishes in no time. No more waiting for the oven to preheat or slow roasting. With the hot air fryer you can have your favorite dishes on the table in just a few minutes.

In addition, the hot air fryer is extremely versatile. Not only can you use it to fry, but you can also grill, roast, bake and even reheat. From crispy French fries to juicy chicken thighs to delicious chocolate chip cookies, the options are endless. With this kitchen appliance you can try out a variety of recipes and let your creativity run wild in the kitchen.

Tips for buying an air fryer

If you are looking for an air fryer, there are a few important things to consider. In this section, we will provide you with useful tips that will help you choose the best air fryer for your needs.

1. Size and Capacity: Before purchasing an air fryer, consider how much space you have in your kitchen and how many people you typically cook for. There are different models with different sizes and capacities, so it is important to choose a deep fryer that meets your needs.

2. Performance and Settings: Pay attention to the performance of the air fryer as it may affect the cooking time of your food. Additionally, the deep fryer should have different settings to prepare different types of food. Some models even offer preset programs for specific dishes.

3. Operation and Cleaning: An easy-to-use air fryer is a must, especially if you are a beginner. Choose a model with an intuitive interface and easy-to-follow instructions. Also check if the deep fryer is easy to clean as this makes maintenance and care easier.

4. Safety features: Look for safety features such as overheat protection, auto shut-off, and non-slip feet. These features ensure that you can use the deep fryer safely and minimize the risk of accidents.

5. Price and guarantee: Compare the prices of different models and pay attention to the price-performance ratio. Also check the warranty terms and conditions to ensure you are covered in the event of a defect or problem.

With these tips, you are now well equipped to choose an air fryer that meets your needs. Enjoy the healthy and delicious meals you can prepare with your new air fryer!

Proper care and cleaning of the hot air fryer

A hot air fryer is a great kitchen aid that allows you to prepare delicious and healthy dishes - without using a lot of oil. To ensure that your hot air fryer always stays in top condition and that you can use it for a long time, regular care and cleaning is essential. In this chapter you will learn how to properly care for and clean your hot air fryer to always achieve the best results.

Caring for your hot air fryer begins before you use it for the first time. Read the user manual carefully to familiarize yourself with the specific care instructions for your device. Make sure you thoroughly clean all removable parts such as the fry basket, container and lid before using them for the first time. Rinse them with warm water and mild detergent and dry them thoroughly before putting them back in place.

After each use, you should clean the air fryer to remove excess food residue. Remove the frying basket and empty it. Clean it thoroughly with warm water and detergent, or use a dishwasher if recommended by the manufacturer. Make sure that no food residue remains in the device, as this can lead to unpleasant odors and impair functionality.

Once a month you should give your hot air fryer a more intensive cleaning. Remove all removable parts and clean them thoroughly. Also check the heating elements for dirt and carefully remove them with a soft cloth. Make sure that there are no cleaning agent residues left behind, as these can produce an unpleasant smell the next time you use it.

By caring for and cleaning your air fryer regularly, you will ensure that it always works perfectly and can conjure up many delicious dishes. Follow the specific care instructions for your device and stick to the recommended cleaning intervals. With the right care, you will be able to enjoy your air fryer for a long time and prepare healthy meals for you and your loved ones.

Chapter 2: Air Fryer Basics

The different parts of an air fryer

In this chapter we will look at the different parts of an air fryer. It's important to understand the function and use of each part to get the most out of your air fryer. An air fryer is a modern kitchen appliance that allows you to prepare low-fat and delicious dishes.

The first part we will look at is the fry basket. This basket is usually removable and is used to hold the food while frying. It is important not to overcrowd the basket to ensure an even and crispy texture. The basket usually has a non-stick coating to prevent food from sticking.

Another important part is the heating element. This part creates the hot air used to fry the food. The temperature can be adjusted depending on the recipe to achieve optimal results. The heating element should be cleaned regularly to ensure optimal performance.

The controls are also an essential part of an air fryer. Here you can set the temperature, set the cooking time and select different programs. Most air fryers have a digital display that shows the settings and remaining cooking time.

Some hot air fryers are also equipped with a stirring arm. This arm mixes the food while frying to ensure even browning and crispiness. This is especially useful when making french fries or other fried foods.

In addition to these main parts, there are also accessories such as baking pans or grill racks that allow you to prepare a variety of dishes in your air fryer. These accessories expand the capabilities of your air fryer and give you even more cooking options.

By understanding the different parts of your air fryer, you can use it effectively and prepare delicious, healthy meals. With the right settings and a little practice, you will quickly become a pro at preparing fried foods.

The operation and settings of the hot air fryer

In this chapter we will familiarize ourselves with the operation and the various settings of your hot air fryer. This knowledge will help you utilize the full capabilities of your deep fryer and prepare delicious meals.

Operating your hot air fryer is incredibly easy. Start by connecting the device to a safe electrical outlet and inserting the plug. Make sure the deep fryer is on a stable and heat-resistant surface.

Before using the deep fryer, it is important that you thoroughly clean the basket and container. This ensures that your dishes are free of unwanted flavors. Be sure to also clean the heating coil and heating element to ensure optimal performance.

After cleaning the deep fryer, you can turn it on. Most models have a digital control panel where you can set the desired temperature and time. Experiment with different temperatures and time settings to find the perfect cooking process for your favorite dishes.

One of the great advantages of the air fryer is that you need to use little or even no oil. However, depending on your recipe, you can add a small drizzle of oil to give your dishes a crispy texture. However, be careful not to use excessive oil as this can lead to an unhealthy result.

Most air fryers have pre-programmed settings for different dishes like french fries, chicken wings, or even cake. These features make it easy for you to prepare delicious meals without having to worry about the right time and temperature.

In this chapter we will also give you some tips and tricks for using your air fryer. Learn how to cook vegetables to perfection, how to keep meat juicy and the best way to clean your deep fryer.

With the right settings and a little practice, you'll be a pro at operating your air fryer in no time. Be inspired by the many healthy and delicious recipes in this book and discover the diverse possibilities that your hot air fryer offers. Have fun cooking!

Safety guidelines when using an air fryer

When cooking with an air fryer, it is important to take proper safety precautions to avoid accidents and achieve the best results. This section introduces some important safety guidelines that will help you use your air fryer safely and prepare delicious meals.

1. Placement and Power: Make sure your air fryer is placed on a stable, flat surface to avoid tipping over during operation. Make sure the power cord is not damaged and that the fryer is properly grounded.

2. Heat Resistant Surfaces: The exterior surface of the air fryer may become very hot during use. Avoid handling the deep fryer without protective gloves to prevent burns. Make sure children and pets are kept away from the deep fryer.

3. Overheat protection: Modern air fryers are equipped with overheat protection that automatically switches off the fryer if the temperature gets too high. However, be careful not to overload the deep fryer and never leave it unattended.

4. Cleaning: Before cleaning your air fryer, make sure it has cooled completely. Use only mild detergents and soft sponges to avoid scratching the surface. Never immerse the device in water.

5. Instruction Manual: Read your air fryer instruction manual carefully to familiarize yourself with the specific safety precautions and operating instructions. Each deep fryer can be slightly different, so it's important to follow the manufacturer's instructions.

Chapter 3: Tips and tricks for perfect results

Set the correct temperature and cooking time

One of the most important factors for the success of your hot air fryer is the correct setting of temperature and cooking time. With this basic information, you will be able to create delicious and perfectly prepared dishes.

Temperature is crucial to achieving the desired texture and flavor of your food. Most air fryers offer a temperature range of 80°C to 200°C, depending on your model. For crispy French fries or fried chicken, we recommend a temperature of 180°C to 200°C. For more delicate foods such as fish or vegetables, lower temperatures of 120°C to 160°C are appropriate. However, feel free to experiment with the temperature settings to suit your personal preferences.

The cooking time depends on the type and size of food you want to prepare. Smaller pieces generally take less time than larger ones. A good rule of thumb is to halve the cooking time when cutting food into smaller pieces. For example, a chicken leg needs around 25-30 minutes at 180°C, while French fries only need 15-20 minutes. It is important to check food regularly during the cooking process to avoid overcooking or burning.

Some air fryers have preset programs for specific dishes that can help you set the correct temperature and cooking time automatically. Check your deep fryer's instruction manual to get the most out of these features.

Keep in mind that each recipe may have its own specific instructions for temperature and cooking time. Therefore, always follow the recipe instructions for optimal results.

With the right setting of temperature and cooking time, you will be able to prepare delicious and healthy dishes in your air fryer. Experiment with different temperatures and cooking times to find your own taste. And don't forget to have fun cooking and enjoy your creations!

Use of oil and spices

Oil and spices are essential components when cooking with the air fryer. They not only add flavor to the dishes, but also have an influence on the consistency and aroma of the food. In this section, you'll learn how to make the most of oil and spices in your recipes to create healthy and delicious dishes.

Oil plays an important role when frying with the air fryer. It helps to make the food crispy and golden brown without requiring a lot of fat. When buying oil, you should choose high-quality options such as olive oil, rapeseed oil or avocado oil. These contain healthy fatty acids and give the dishes a natural taste. Avoid using oils with a low smoke point as they can burn quickly when fried and leave an unpleasant taste.

Spices are the secret to adding the finishing touch to air fryer dishes. Using a variety of spices, you can add unique flavors to your dishes and combine different flavors. Popular spices for the air fryer include paprika, garlic powder, onion powder, cumin, oregano and thyme. Experiment with different spice combinations to give your dishes a personal touch.

It's important to use the right amount of oil and spices so as not to overwhelm the flavor of your dishes. Start with small amounts and add more if necessary. Remember that spices release their flavors during the cooking process, so it is advisable to add them early.

In this book you will find a variety of healthy and delicious recipes for beginners and professionals, all illustrated with beautiful color pictures. You will also receive useful tips and tricks to get the most out of your air fryer. Be inspired by the recipes and discover the many possibilities that using oil and spices in the hot air fryer offers.

Variations and adjustments to the recipes

In this section of the book "The Large Air Fryer Recipe Book: Healthy and Delicious Dishes for Every Taste" we will look at the variations and adaptations of the recipes. We understand that not everyone's tastes are the same and that everyone has their own culinary preferences. That's why we've put together a variety of recipes that are suitable for both beginners and professionals.

One of the great features of the air fryer is its versatility. Not only can you prepare French fries and chicken legs, but also a variety of other dishes. With a few small adjustments you can adapt the recipes to your taste and add your own personal touches.

For example, you can swap out spices and herbs to adjust the flavor. If the recipe uses paprika, you could use cayenne pepper instead for a spicier flavor. Or add fresh herbs like basil or cilantro for a fresh and aromatic kick.

You can also vary the ingredients to tailor the dish to your preferences. If the recipe uses chicken, you could use salmon or tofu instead to make it vegetarian or pescatarian. Experiment with different vegetables to vary the color and flavor of the dish.

In addition, in this book you will find many tips and tricks on how to adapt the recipes to make them healthier. We offer alternative preparation methods to reduce the calorie content and give you suggestions for nutrient-dense ingredients you can add to increase the health value.

Whether you are a beginner or a professional, this book offers many healthy and delicious recipes illustrated with beautiful color pictures. You will surely find inspiration and expand your culinary skills. So, let your creativity run wild and discover the many possibilities of variations and adjustments to recipes with your air fryer!

Troubleshooting Air Fryer Issues

In this section, we will look at common problems when using an air fryer and provide you with practical troubleshooting solutions. The goal is to help you ensure a smooth and successful cooking experience so you can enjoy your healthy and delicious dishes without frustration.

1. The air fryer is not heating up properly:- Check that the socket is working and that the device is plugged in properly.- Make sure that the temperature control is set correctly and that the desired temperature is reached.- Check that the basket and the inside of the deep fryer is clean, as contamination can affect performance.

2. Food doesn't get crispy:- Make sure you spread the food evenly in the basket so that the hot air reaches all sides.- Only use a thin layer of oil or cooking spray to spray the food as too much Fat that can prevent crisping.- Be careful not to put too much food in the fryer at the same time as this can lead to overcrowding and the result will be less crispy.

3. Smoke:- Check for grease or residue build-up in the bottom of the fryer. Clean the device thoroughly to avoid smoke.- Make sure you do not put oily or greasy food in the fryer as this can cause smoke.

With these simple troubleshooting tips, you should be able to solve the most common problems when using your air fryer. Remember that practice makes perfect and you will get better over time. Enjoy your culinary adventures and discover the variety of healthy and delicious dishes you can prepare with your air fryer!

QUICK SNACKS

1. Crispy cheese sticks

★★★★☆

🕐 10 Minuten   ♨🕐 6 Minuten   🍴 4 servings

INGREDIENTS

- 8 mozzarella sticks
- 1 cup breadcrumbs
- 1/2 cup grated Parmesan cheese
- 2 eggs, beaten
- Salt and pepper to taste

INSTRUCTIONS

1. Preheat the air fryer to 400°F (200°C).
2. Cut the mozzarella sticks in half to make 16 shorter sticks.
3. In a shallow dish, mix breadcrumbs, Parmesan cheese, salt, and pepper.
4. Dip each mozzarella stick in beaten eggs, then coat with breadcrumb mixture.
5. Place the coated sticks in the air fryer basket in a single layer.
6. Air fry for 5-6 minutes until golden and crispy.
7. Serve hot with marinara sauce for dipping.

Nutritional Data: 240 calories | 15g carbs | 12g protein | 14g fat | 1g fiber | 1g sugar

2. Vegetable Chips

★★★★★

🕐 15 Minuten   ♨🕐 10 Minuten   🍴 4 servings

INGREDIENTS

- 2 large potatoes
- 2 large carrots
- 1 zucchini
- 2 tablespoons olive oil
- Salt and pepper to taste Instructions:

INSTRUCTIONS

1. Wash and peel the vegetables. Using a mandoline slicer, thinly slice the potatoes, carrots, and zucchini.
2. Pat dry the slices with a paper towel to remove excess moisture.
3. In a bowl, toss the vegetable slices with olive oil, salt, and pepper until evenly coated.
4. Preheat the air fryer to 375°F (190°C).
5. Arrange the vegetable slices in a single layer in the air fryer basket.
6. Air fry for 10-12 minutes, flipping halfway through, until crispy and golden brown.
7. Serve immediately as a healthy snack or side dish.

Nutritional Data | Calories: 120 | Fat: 7g | Carbohydrates: 13g | Protein: 2g | Fiber: 3g | Sodium: 200mg

3.Chicken Nuggets

★★★★★

⏱ 20 Minuten   🍳⏱ 12Minuten   🍴 4 servings

INGREDIENTS

- 1 lb boneless, skinless chicken breasts, cut into bite-sized pieces
- 1 cup breadcrumbs
- 1/2 cup grated Parmesan cheese
- 2 eggs, beaten
- Salt and pepper to taste

INSTRUCTIONS

1. Preheat the air fryer to 400°F (200°C).
2. In a shallow dish, mix breadcrumbs, Parmesan cheese, salt, and pepper.
3. Dip each chicken piece in beaten eggs, then coat with breadcrumb mixture.
4. Place the coated chicken nuggets in the air fryer basket in a single layer.
5. Air fry for 10-12 minutes, flipping halfway through, until golden and cooked through.
6. Serve hot with your favorite dipping sauce.

Nutritional Data: 280 calories | 18g carbs | 28g protein | 10g fat | 1g fiber | 1g sugar

4.Shrimp with Garlic and Lemon

★★★★★

⏱ 15 Minuten   🍳⏱ 8 Minuten   🍴 4 servings

INGREDIENTS

- 1 lb large shrimp, peeled and deveined
- 4 cloves garlic, minced
- 2 tablespoons olive oil
- Zest and juice of 1 lemon
- Salt and pepper to taste
- Fresh parsley for garnish

INSTRUCTIONS

1. In a bowl, toss the shrimp with minced garlic, olive oil, lemon zest, lemon juice, salt, and pepper until evenly coated.
2. Preheat the air fryer to 400°F (200°C).
3. Place the seasoned shrimp in the air fryer basket in a single layer.
4. Air fry for 6-8 minutes until the shrimp are pink and cooked through.
5. Garnish with chopped parsley before serving.
6. Serve hot as an appetizer or over pasta or rice for a main dish.

Nutritional Data | Calories: 180 | Fat: 8g | Carbohydrates: 2g | Protein: 24g | Fiber: 0g | Sodium: 300mg

5. Mozzarella Balls

★★★★

🕐 15 Minuten   🍳🕐 15 Minuten   🍴 4 servings

INGREDIENTS

- 16 small mozzarella balls
- 1 cup breadcrumbs
- 1/2 cup grated Parmesan cheese
- 2 eggs, beaten
- Salt and pepper to taste

INSTRUCTIONS

1. Preheat the air fryer to 400°F (200°C).
2. In a shallow dish, mix breadcrumbs, Parmesan cheese, salt, and pepper.
3. Dip each mozzarella ball in beaten eggs, then coat with breadcrumb mixture.
4. Place the coated mozzarella balls in the air fryer basket in a single layer.
5. Air fry for 5-6 minutes until golden and crispy.
6. Serve hot with marinara sauce for dipping.

Nutritional Data | Calories: 250 | Fat: 15g | Carbohydrates: 14g | Protein: 16g | Fiber: 1g | Sodium: 400mg

6. Apple Cinnamon Chips

★★★★★

🕐 10 Minuten   🍳🕐 10 Minuten   🍴 4 servings

INGREDIENTS

- 2 large apples, cored and thinly sliced
- 1 tablespoon cinnamon
- 1 tablespoon sugar (optional)

INSTRUCTIONS

1. Preheat the air fryer to 375°F (190°C).
2. In a bowl, toss the apple slices with cinnamon and sugar (if using) until evenly coated.
3. Arrange the apple slices in a single layer in the air fryer basket.
4. Air fry for 10-12 minutes until crispy and lightly browned.
5. Let cool slightly before serving.
6. Serve as a healthy snack or dessert.

Nutritional Data| Calories: 80 | Fat: 0g | Carbohydrates: 21g | Protein: 0g | Fiber: 3g | Sodium: 0mg

7. Mini Pizza Pockets

★★★★★

🕐 15 Minuten   ♨🕐 10 Minuten   🍴 4 servings

INSTRUCTIONS

1. Preheat the air fryer to 375°F (190°C).
2. Roll out the pizza dough and cut into small squares.
3. Place a spoonful of pizza sauce, shredded mozzarella cheese, pepperoni, olives, bell peppers, and onions on each square.
4. Fold the dough over the filling to create mini pockets and seal the edges with a fork.
5. Brush the tops of the pockets with beaten egg.
6. Place the pizza pockets in the air fryer basket in a single layer.
7. Air fry for 8-10 minutes until golden and crispy.
8. Serve hot with additional pizza sauce for dipping.

INGREDIENTS

- 1 package refrigerated pizza dough
- 1/2 cup pizza sauce
- 1 cup shredded mozzarella cheese
- 1/4 cup sliced pepperoni
- 1/4 cup sliced black olives
- 1/4 cup diced bell peppers
- 1/4 cup diced onions
- 1 egg, beaten

Nutritional Data: 320 calories | 25g carbs | 14g protein | 18g fat | 2g fiber | 3g sugar

8. Spicy Chickpeas

★★★★★

🕐 5 Minuten   ♨🕐 15 Minuten   🍴 4 servings

INSTRUCTIONS

1. Preheat the air fryer to 375°F (190°C).
2. In a bowl, toss the chickpeas with olive oil, paprika, cayenne pepper, and salt until evenly coated.
3. Place the seasoned chickpeas in the air fryer basket.
4. Air fry for 12-15 minutes until crispy, shaking the basket halfway through.
5. Let cool slightly before serving.
6. Serve as a crunchy snack or salad topper.

INGREDIENTS

- 2 cans chickpeas, drained and rinsed
- 2 tablespoons olive oil
- 1 tablespoon paprika
- 1 teaspoon cayenne pepper
- Salt to taste

Nutritional Data: 220 calories | 30g carbs | 8g protein | 10g fat | 8g fiber | 5g sugar

9.Fish Fingers

★★★★★

🕐 15 Minuten   ♨🕐 10 Minuten   🍴 4 servings

INGREDIENTS

- 1 lb white fish fillets (such as cod or haddock), cut into strips
- 1 cup breadcrumbs
- 1/2 cup grated Parmesan cheese
- 2 eggs, beaten
- Salt and pepper to taste

INSTRUCTIONS

1. Preheat the air fryer to 400°F (200°C).
2. In a shallow dish, mix breadcrumbs, Parmesan cheese, salt, and pepper.
3. Dip each fish strip in beaten eggs, then coat with breadcrumb mixture.
4. Place the coated fish strips in the air fryer basket in a single layer.
5. Air fry for 8-10 minutes until golden and crispy.
6. Serve hot with tartar sauce or lemon wedges.

Nutritional Data | Calories: 280 | Fat: 8g | Carbohydrates: 18g | Protein: 32g | Fiber: 1g | Sodium: 400mg

10.Olive Cheese Balls

★★★★

🕐 15 Minuten   ♨🕐 10 Minuten   🍴 4 servings

INGREDIENTS

- 1 cup shredded mozzarella cheese
- 1/4 cup grated Parmesan cheese
- 1/4 cup chopped black olives
- 1/4 cup chopped fresh parsley
- 1/2 teaspoon garlic powder
- 1/2 teaspoon dried oregano
- Salt and pepper to taste

INSTRUCTIONS

1. In a bowl, mix together mozzarella cheese, Parmesan cheese, black olives, parsley, garlic powder, oregano, salt, and pepper until well combined.
2. Form the mixture into small balls and place them on a parchment-lined tray.
3. Preheat the air fryer to 375°F (190°C).
4. Place the olive cheese balls in the air fryer basket in a single layer.
5. Air fry for 8-10 minutes until golden and melted.
6. Serve hot as a delicious appetizer or snack.

Nutritional Data: 200 calories | 5g carbs | 15g protein | 14g fat | 2g fiber | 1g sugar

11. Cinnamon Apple Granola with Almonds

★★★★★

🕐 10 Minuten   🍳🕐 20 Minuten   🍴 6 servings

INGREDIENTS

- 3 cups rolled oats
- 1 cup chopped almonds
- 1/4 cup honey
- 2 tablespoons coconut oil, melted
- 1 teaspoon ground cinnamon
- 1/2 teaspoon vanilla extract
- 1 cup dried apple slices

INSTRUCTIONS

1. Preheat the air fryer to 300°F (150°C).
2. In a bowl, mix together rolled oats, chopped almonds, honey, melted coconut oil, cinnamon, and vanilla extract until well combined.
3. Spread the granola mixture evenly on the air fryer basket.
4. Air fry for 15-20 minutes, stirring halfway through, until golden and crisp.
5. Let the granola cool completely before adding dried apple slices.
6. Store in an airtight container for up to two weeks.
7. Serve with yogurt or milk for breakfast or as a healthy snack.

Nutritional Data: 280 calories | 35g carbs | 7g protein | 14g fat | 5g fiber | 15g sugar

12. Protein-Rich Lentil Crunchies

★★★★★

🕐 15 Minuten   🍳🕐 20 Minuten   🍴 4 servings

INGREDIENTS

- 1 cup cooked lentils
- 1/4 cup breadcrumbs
- 1/4 cup grated Parmesan cheese
- 1 egg, beaten
- 1 tablespoon olive oil
- 1 teaspoon garlic powder
- 1 teaspoon smoked paprika
- Salt and pepper to taste

INSTRUCTIONS

1. Preheat the air fryer to 375°F (190°C).
2. In a food processor, pulse cooked lentils until they form a coarse paste.
3. Transfer the lentil paste to a bowl and mix in breadcrumbs, Parmesan cheese, beaten egg, olive oil, garlic powder, smoked paprika, salt, and pepper until well combined.
4. Shape the mixture into small patties or nuggets.
5. Place the lentil crunchies in the air fryer basket in a single layer.
6. Air fry for 20-25 minutes, flipping halfway through, until golden and crispy.
7. Serve hot with your favorite dipping sauce or on top of salads.

Nutritional Data: 220 calories | 20g carbs | 12g protein | 10g fat | 5g fiber | 2g sugar

13. Golden Turmeric Cashew Granola

★★★★

🕐 10 Minuten   🍳🕐 20Minuten   🍴 6 servings

INGREDIENTS

- 3 cups rolled oats
- 1 cup cashews
- 1/4 cup honey
- 2 tablespoons coconut oil, melted
- 1 teaspoon ground turmeric
- 1/2 teaspoon ground ginger
- 1/2 teaspoon ground cinnamon
- 1/4 teaspoon ground black pepper
- 1/2 cup dried cranberries

INSTRUCTIONS

1. Preheat the air fryer to 300°F (150°C).
2. In a bowl, mix together rolled oats, cashews, honey, melted coconut oil, turmeric, ginger, cinnamon, and black pepper until well combined.
3. Spread the granola mixture evenly on the air fryer basket.
4. Air fry for 15-20 minutes, stirring halfway through, until golden and crisp.
5. Let the granola cool completely before adding dried cranberries.
6. Store in an airtight container for up to two weeks.
7. Serve with yogurt or milk for breakfast or as a healthy snack.

Nutritional Data: 320 calories | 40g carbs | 7g protein | 16g fat | 5g fiber | 20g sugar

14. Crunchy Soybeans with Sea Salt

★★★★★

🕐 5 Minuten   🍳🕐 15 Minuten   🍴 4 servings

INGREDIENTS

- 2 cups frozen edamame (soybeans), thawed
- 1 tablespoon olive oil
- Sea salt to taste

INSTRUCTIONS

1. Preheat the air fryer to 375°F (190°C).
2. In a bowl, toss the thawed edamame with olive oil until evenly coated.
3. Spread the edamame in a single layer in the air fryer basket.
4. Air fry for 12-15 minutes until crispy, shaking the basket halfway through.
5. Sprinkle with sea salt before serving.
6. Serve hot as a nutritious snack or appetizer.

Nutritional Data: 160 calories | 10g carbs | 12g protein | 8g fat | 6g fiber | 2g sugar

15. Spicy Black Bean Crisps

★★★★★

🕐 10 Minuten   ♨🕐 15 Minuten   🍴 4 servings

INGREDIENTS

- 1 can black beans, drained and rinsed
- 1 tablespoon olive oil
- 1 teaspoon chili powder
- 1/2 teaspoon cumin
- 1/2 teaspoon garlic powder
- Salt to taste

INSTRUCTIONS

1. Preheat the air fryer to 375°F (190°C).
2. In a bowl, toss the black beans with olive oil, chili powder, cumin, garlic powder, and salt until evenly coated.
3. Spread the seasoned black beans in a single layer in the air fryer basket.
4. Air fry for 12-15 minutes until crispy, shaking the basket halfway through.
5. Let cool slightly before serving.
6. Serve as a crunchy snack or salad topper.

Nutritional Data: 180 calories | 20g carbs | 8g protein | 8g fat | 6g fiber | 1g sugar

16. Spicy Chickpea Snack Bites

★★★★★

🕐 10 Minuten   ♨🕐 15 Minuten   🍴 4 servings

INGREDIENTS

- 2 cans chickpeas, drained and rinsed
- 1 tablespoon olive oil
- 1 teaspoon chili powder
- 1/2 teaspoon cumin
- 1/2 teaspoon garlic powder
- Salt to taste

INSTRUCTIONS

1. Preheat the air fryer to 375°F (190°C).
2. In a bowl, toss the chickpeas with olive oil, chili powder, cumin, garlic powder, and salt until evenly coated.
3. Spread the seasoned chickpeas in a single layer in the air fryer basket.
4. Air fry for 12-15 minutes until crispy, shaking the basket halfway through.
5. Let cool slightly before serving.
6. Serve as a crunchy snack or salad topper.

Nutritional Data: 220 calories | 25g carbs | 10g protein | 10g fat | 8g fiber | 2g sugar

BREAKFAST

17. Airy French Toast Sticks

★★★★

🕐 10 Minuten   〰🕐 8 Minuten   🍴 4 servings

INGREDIENTS

- 8 slices bread, cut into strips
- 2 eggs
- 1/4 cup milk
- 1 teaspoon vanilla extract
- 1/2 teaspoon ground cinnamon
- Maple syrup for serving

INSTRUCTIONS

1. In a shallow dish, whisk together eggs, milk, vanilla extract, and cinnamon.
2. Dip each bread strip into the egg mixture, coating evenly.
3. Preheat the air fryer to 350°F (175°C).
4. Place the coated bread strips in the air fryer basket in a single layer.
5. Air fry for 6-8 minutes until golden and crispy.
6. Serve hot with maple syrup for dipping.

Nutritional Data | Calories: 300 | Protein: 12g | Carbohydrates: 45g | Fat: 9g | Fiber: 2g | Sodium: 400mg

18. Mini Breakfast Quiches

★★★★★

🕐 15 Minuten   〰🕐 12 Minuten   🍴 4 servings

INSTRUCTIONS

1. Preheat the air fryer to 350°F (175°C).
2. In a bowl, whisk together eggs, milk, salt, and pepper.
3. Stir in shredded cheese, diced ham or bacon, and diced bell peppers.
4. Grease muffin tin cups with cooking spray.
5. Pour the egg mixture evenly into the muffin tin cups.
6. Place the muffin tin in the air fryer basket.
7. Air fry for 10-12 minutes until the quiches are set and golden on top.
8. Let cool slightly before serving.
9. Serve hot or at room temperature as a quick breakfast or brunch option.

INGREDIENTS

- 4 eggs
- 1/4 cup milk
- 1/2 cup shredded cheese
- 1/4 cup diced ham or bacon
- 1/4 cup diced bell peppers
- Salt and pepper to taste

Nutritional Data: 220 calories | 3g carbs | 14g protein | 17g fat | 1g fiber | 1g sugar

19. Crispy Bacon Strips

★★★★

🕐 5 Minuten   ♨🕐 10 Minuten   🍴 2 servings

INGREDIENTS

- 8 slices bacon

INSTRUCTIONS

1. Preheat the air fryer to 400°F (200°C).
2. Place bacon slices in a single layer in the air fryer basket.
3. Air fry for 8-10 minutes until crispy, flipping halfway through.
4. Remove from the air fryer and drain on paper towels.
5. Serve hot as a breakfast side or use in sandwiches and salads.

Nutritional Data: 240 calories | 0g carbs | 12g protein | 20g fat | 0g fiber | 0g sugar

20. Sweet Potato Rosti

★★★★

🕐 15 Minuten   ♨🕐 15 Minuten   🍴 4 servings

INSTRUCTIONS

1. In a bowl, mix together grated sweet potatoes, chopped onion, salt, and pepper.
2. Heat olive oil in a skillet over medium heat.
3. Divide the sweet potato mixture into 4 portions and shape each portion into a patty.
4. Cook the rosti patties in the skillet for 6-8 minutes on each side until golden and crispy.
5. Preheat the air fryer to 375°F (190°C).
6. Place the cooked rosti patties in the air fryer basket.
7. Air fry for 5-7 minutes until heated through and extra crispy.
8. Serve hot as a side dish or breakfast hash.

INGREDIENTS

- 2 large sweet potatoes, peeled and grated
- 1 small onion, finely chopped
- 2 tablespoons olive oil
- Salt and pepper to taste

Nutritional Data | Calories: 180 | Protein: 4g | Carbohydrates: 30g | Fat: 5g | Fiber: 4g | Sodium: 600mg

21. Apple Cinnamon Muffins

★★★★

🕐 15 Minuten   🍳🕐 20 Minuten   🍴 12 servings

INGREDIENTS

- 2 cups all-purpose flour
- 1/2 cup sugar
- 2 teaspoons baking powder
- 1/2 teaspoon baking soda
- 1/2 teaspoon salt
- 1 teaspoon ground cinnamon
- 1/4 cup unsalted butter, melted
- 2 eggs
- 1 cup unsweetened applesauce
- 1 teaspoon vanilla extract
- 1 cup diced apples

INSTRUCTIONS

1. Preheat the air fryer to 350°F (175°C).
2. In a large bowl, whisk together flour, sugar, baking powder, baking soda, salt, and cinnamon.
3. In another bowl, mix melted butter, eggs, applesauce, and vanilla extract.
4. Pour the wet ingredients into the dry ingredients and stir until just combined.
5. Fold in diced apples.
6. Line muffin cups with paper liners and fill each cup 2/3 full with batter.
7. Place the muffin tin in the air fryer basket.
8. Air fry for 18-22 minutes until a toothpick inserted into the center comes out clean.
9. Let cool in the muffin tin for 5 minutes before transferring to a wire rack to cool completely.
10. Serve warm or at room temperature.

Nutritional Data: 180 calories | 30g carbs | 3g protein | 5g fat | 1g fiber | 15g sugar

22. Banana Nut Bread

★★★★

🕐 15 Minuten   🍳🕐 50 Minuten   🍴 8 servings

INSTRUCTIONS

1. Preheat the air fryer to 325°F (160°C).
2. In a mixing bowl, combine mashed bananas, melted butter, sugar, beaten egg, and vanilla extract.
3. In another bowl, sift together flour, baking soda, and salt.
4. Gradually add the dry ingredients to the wet ingredients and mix until just combined.
5. Fold in chopped nuts.
6. Grease a loaf pan with cooking spray and pour the batter into the pan.
7. Place the loaf pan in the air fryer basket.
8. Air fry for 45-50 minutes until a toothpick inserted into the center comes out clean.
9. Let cool in the pan for 10 minutes before transferring to a wire rack to cool completely.
10. Slice and serve warm or at room temperature.

INGREDIENTS

- 2 ripe bananas, mashed
- 1/3 cup melted butter
- 3/4 cup sugar
- 1 egg, beaten
- 1 teaspoon vanilla extract
- 1 1/2 cups all-purpose flour
- 1 teaspoon baking soda
- 1/2 teaspoon salt
- 1/2 cup chopped nuts (such as walnuts or pecans)

Nutritional Data: 280 calories | 40g carbs | 5g protein | 12g fat | 2g fiber | 20g sugar

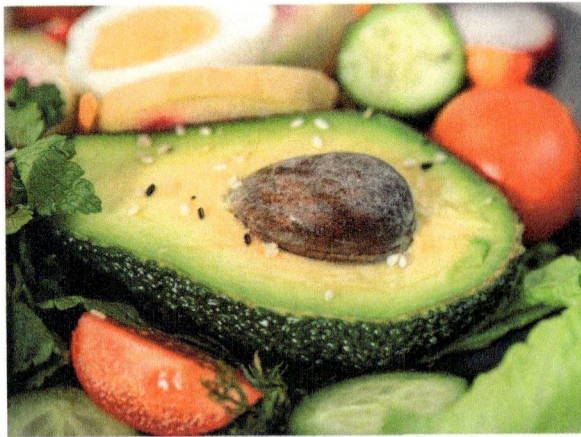

23.Avocado "Fries"

★★★★

🕐 10 Minuten   ♨🕐 10 Minuten   🍴 4 servings

INSTRUCTIONS

1. Preheat the air fryer to 400°F (200°C).
2. Set up a breading station with three shallow dishes: one with flour, one with beaten eggs, and one with breadcrumbs mixed with Parmesan cheese, salt, and pepper.
3. Dredge avocado slices in flour, shaking off excess.
4. Dip in beaten eggs, then coat with breadcrumb mixture.
5. Place the coated avocado slices in the air fryer basket in a single layer.
6. Air fry for 8-10 minutes until golden and crispy.
7. Serve hot with your favorite dipping sauce.

INGREDIENTS

- 2 ripe avocados, sliced into wedges
- 1/2 cup all-purpose flour
- 2 eggs, beaten
- 1 cup breadcrumbs
- 1/2 cup grated Parmesan cheese
- Salt and pepper to taste

Nutritional Data: 220 calories | 20g carbs | 8g protein | 14g fat | 5g fiber | 2g sugar

24.Omelette Cubes

★★★★

🕐 10 Minuten   ♨🕐 10 Minuten   🍴 4 servings

INSTRUCTIONS

1. In a bowl, whisk together eggs, milk, salt, and pepper.
2. Stir in diced ham or bacon, diced bell peppers, diced onions, and shredded cheese.
3. Preheat the air fryer to 350°F (175°C).
4. Pour the egg mixture into a greased baking dish that fits into the air fryer basket.
5. Air fry for 8-10 minutes until the eggs are set and slightly golden on top.
6. Let cool slightly before cutting into cubes.
7. Serve hot or at room temperature as a protein-packed breakfast or snack.

INGREDIENTS

- 6 eggs
- 1/4 cup milk
- 1/2 cup diced ham or cooked bacon
- 1/4 cup diced bell peppers
- 1/4 cup diced onions
- 1/2 cup shredded cheese
- Salt and pepper to taste

Nutritional Data: 280 calories | 5g carbs | 20g protein | 20g fat | 1g fiber | 2g sugar

25. Egg and Ham Breakfast Wrap

★★★★

🕐 **10 Minuten**　　🍳🕐 **5 Minuten**　　🍴 **2 servings**

INGREDIENTS

- 4 large eggs
- 2 tablespoons milk
- Salt and pepper to taste
- 4 slices ham
- 2 large flour tortillas
- 1/2 cup shredded cheese
- Salsa or hot sauce for serving (optional)

INSTRUCTIONS

1. In a bowl, whisk together eggs, milk, salt, and pepper.
2. Heat a skillet over medium heat and scramble the eggs until cooked through.
3. Warm the tortillas in the microwave or skillet.
4. Place 2 slices of ham on each tortilla.
5. Divide scrambled eggs and shredded cheese evenly between the tortillas.
6. Fold the sides of the tortillas over the filling and roll up tightly to form wraps.
7. Preheat the air fryer to 350°F (175°C).
8. Place the wraps in the air fryer basket seam-side down.
9. Air fry for 4-5 minutes until the tortillas are crispy and golden.
10. Serve hot with salsa or hot sauce if desired.

Nutritional Data: 320 calories | 20g carbs | 25g protein | 15g fat | 2g fiber | 1g sugar

26. Greek Spinach and Feta Packets

★★★★

🕐 **20 Minuten**　　🍳🕐 **15 Minuten**　　🍴 **4 servings**

INGREDIENTS

- 1 tablespoon olive oil
- 1 onion, finely chopped
- 2 cloves garlic, minced
- 1 bunch spinach, chopped
- 1/2 cup crumbled feta cheese
- Salt and pepper to taste
- 8 sheets phyllo dough
- Cooking spray

INSTRUCTIONS

1. Heat olive oil in a skillet over medium heat. Add chopped onion and minced garlic, and cook until softened.
2. Add chopped spinach to the skillet and cook until wilted. Remove from heat and let cool slightly.
3. Stir in crumbled feta cheese, salt, and pepper.
4. Preheat the air fryer to 375°F (190°C).
5. Lay out one sheet of phyllo dough and brush lightly with olive oil or spray with cooking spray.
6. Place another sheet of phyllo dough on top and repeat the process until you have 4 layers.
7. Cut the layered phyllo dough into squares.
8. Place a spoonful of the spinach and feta mixture in the center of each square.
9. Fold the edges of the phyllo dough over the filling to form packets.
10. Place the packets in the air fryer basket in a single layer.
11. Air fry for 12-15 minutes until the packets are golden and crispy.
12. Serve hot as a delicious appetizer or side dish.

Nutritional Data: 240 calories | 20g carbs | 8g protein | 15g fat | 2g fiber | 2g sugar

27. Chia Yogurt Pots

★★★

🕐 **15 Minuten**   ⏲ **5 Minuten**   🍴 **2 servings**

INSTRUCTIONS

1. In a bowl, mix together Greek yogurt, chia seeds, and honey or maple syrup.
2. Divide the mixture into two small jars or cups.
3. Cover and refrigerate for at least 2 hours or overnight to allow the chia seeds to thicken the yogurt.
4. Before serving, top with fresh fruit, granola, or nuts for added flavor and texture.
5. Serve chilled as a nutritious breakfast or snack option.

INGREDIENTS

- • 1 cup Greek yogurt
- 2 tablespoons chia seeds
- 1 tablespoon honey or maple syrup
- Fresh fruit, granola, or nuts for topping

Nutritional Data: 200 calories | 20g carbs | 15g protein | 8g fat | 5g fiber | 10g sugar

28. Vegetable and Cheese Bagels

★★★★

🕐 **10 Minuten**   ⏲ **5 Minuten**   🍴 **2 servings**

INSTRUCTIONS

1. Preheat the air fryer to 350°F (175°C).
2. Spread cream cheese on the bottom halves of the bagels.
3. Top with sliced vegetables and shredded cheese.
4. Season with salt and pepper to taste.
5. Place the bagel halves in the air fryer basket.
6. Air fry for 4-5 minutes until the cheese is melted and bubbly.
7. Remove from the air fryer and assemble the bagels.
8. Serve hot as a quick and satisfying breakfast or lunch option.

INGREDIENTS

- 2 bagels, halved
- 4 tablespoons cream cheese
- 1/2 cup sliced vegetables (such as cucumber, tomato, bell pepper)
- 1/2 cup shredded cheese
- Salt and pepper to taste

Nutritional Data: 320 calories | 40g carbs | 15g protein | 12g fat | 3g fiber | 5g sugar

29. Peach and Curd Tartlets

★★★★

🕐 20 Minuten   ♨🕐 10 Minuten   🍴 4 servings

INSTRUCTIONS

1. Preheat the air fryer to 375°F (190°C).
2. Roll out the thawed puff pastry sheet and cut it into 6 equal squares.
3. Place the pastry squares in the wells of a muffin tin, pressing gently to form tartlet shells.
4. Prick the bottom of each tartlet shell with a fork to prevent puffing.
5. Bake in the preheated air fryer for 10-12 minutes until golden brown and puffed.
6. Let the tartlet shells cool slightly, then remove them from the muffin tin.
7. Fill each tartlet shell with a spoonful of lemon curd.
8. Arrange sliced peaches on top of the curd.
9. Drizzle honey over the tartlets and garnish with fresh mint leaves.
10. Serve warm or at room temperature as a delightful dessert or brunch treat.

INGREDIENTS

- 1 sheet frozen puff pastry, thawed
- 1/2 cup lemon curd
- 2 ripe peaches, thinly sliced
- 2 tablespoons honey
- Fresh mint leaves for garnish

Nutritional Data: 220 calories | 30g carbs | 3g protein | 10g fat | 1g fiber | 15g sugar

30. Granular Energy Balls

★★★★

🕐 15 Minuten   ♨🕐 0 Minuten   🍴 12 servings

INSTRUCTIONS

1. In a mixing bowl, combine rolled oats, almond butter, honey or maple syrup, shredded coconut, chocolate chips or dried fruit, chia seeds, vanilla extract, and a pinch of salt.
2. Stir until well combined and the mixture holds together.
3. Using your hands, roll the mixture into small balls, about 1 inch in diameter.
4. Place the energy balls on a baking sheet lined with parchment paper.
5. Refrigerate for at least 30 minutes to firm up.
6. Serve chilled as a quick and nutritious snack on the go.

INGREDIENTS

- 1 cup rolled oats
- 1/2 cup almond butter
- 1/4 cup honey or maple syrup
- 1/4 cup shredded coconut
- 1/4 cup mini chocolate chips or dried fruit
- 1 tablespoon chia seeds
- 1 teaspoon vanilla extract
- Pinch of salt

Nutritional Data: 140 calories | 15g carbs | 3g protein | 8g fat | 2g fiber | 8g sugar

31. Crunchy Quinoa Power Muesli

★★★★★

🕐 10 Minuten   🍳🕐 20 Minuten   🍴 6 servings

INGREDIENTS

- 1 cup rolled oats
- 1/2 cup quinoa, rinsed and drained
- 1/4 cup almonds, chopped
- 1/4 cup pumpkin seeds
- 1/4 cup shredded coconut
- 2 tablespoons honey or maple syrup
- 2 tablespoons coconut oil, melted
- 1 teaspoon vanilla extract
- Pinch of salt

INSTRUCTIONS

1. Preheat the air fryer to 300°F (150°C).
2. In a large bowl, combine rolled oats, quinoa, chopped almonds, pumpkin seeds, shredded coconut, honey or maple syrup, melted coconut oil, vanilla extract, and a pinch of salt. Mix well.
3. Spread the mixture evenly on the air fryer basket.
4. Air fry for 15-20 minutes, stirring occasionally, until golden brown and crispy.
5. Let cool completely before serving or storing in an airtight container.
6. Serve with yogurt, milk, or as a topping for smoothie bowls.

Nutritional Data: 220 calories | 25g carbs | 6g protein | 12g fat | 4g fiber | 10g sugar

32. Tropical Coconut Oatmeal Granola

★★★★★

🕐 10 Minuten   🍳🕐 20 Minuten   🍴 6 servings

INGREDIENTS

- 2 cups rolled oats
- 1/2 cup shredded coconut
- 1/4 cup chopped almonds
- 1/4 cup chopped dried pineapple
- 1/4 cup chopped dried mango
- 2 tablespoons honey or maple syrup
- 2 tablespoons coconut oil, melted
- 1 teaspoon vanilla extract
- Pinch of salt

INSTRUCTIONS

1. Preheat the air fryer to 300°F (150°C).
2. In a large bowl, combine rolled oats, shredded coconut, chopped almonds, chopped dried pineapple, chopped dried mango, honey or maple syrup, melted coconut oil, vanilla extract, and a pinch of salt. Mix well.
3. Spread the mixture evenly on the air fryer basket.
4. Air fry for 15-20 minutes, stirring occasionally, until golden brown and crispy.
5. Let cool completely before serving or storing in an airtight container.
6. Serve with yogurt, milk, or as a topping for smoothie bowls.

Nutritional Data: 260 calories | 30g carbs | 5g protein | 15g fat | 4g fiber | 15g sugar

33. Chocolate Nut Muesli Clusters

★★★★★

🕐 10 Minuten   ♨🕐 20 Minuten   🍴 8 servings

INGREDIENTS

- 2 cups rolled oats
- 1/2 cup chopped nuts (such as almonds, walnuts, or pecans)
- 1/4 cup unsweetened cocoa powder
- 1/4 cup honey or maple syrup
- 2 tablespoons coconut oil, melted
- 1 teaspoon vanilla extract
- Pinch of salt

INSTRUCTIONS

1. Preheat the air fryer to 300°F (150°C).
2. In a large bowl, mix together rolled oats, chopped nuts, cocoa powder, honey or maple syrup, melted coconut oil, vanilla extract, and a pinch of salt until well combined.
3. Spread the mixture evenly on the air fryer basket.
4. Air fry for 15-20 minutes, stirring occasionally, until golden brown and crispy.
5. Let cool completely before serving or storing in an airtight container.
6. Serve as a delicious and satisfying breakfast cereal or snack.

Nutritional Data: 240 calories | 25g carbs | 5g protein | 12g fat | 4g fiber | 12g sugar

34. Berry Dreams Muesli Mix

★★★★

🕐 10 Minuten   ♨🕐 15 Minuten   🍴 4 servings

INGREDIENTS

- 2 cups rolled oats
- 1/2 cup mixed dried berries (such as strawberries, blueberries, raspberries)
- 1/4 cup chopped nuts (such as almonds, pecans, or walnuts)
- 2 tablespoons chia seeds
- 2 tablespoons honey or maple syrup
- 1 tablespoon coconut oil, melted
- 1 teaspoon vanilla extract
- Pinch of salt

INSTRUCTIONS

1. In a large bowl, combine rolled oats, mixed dried berries, chopped nuts, chia seeds, honey or maple syrup, melted coconut oil, vanilla extract, and a pinch of salt.
2. Stir until everything is evenly coated.
3. Store in an airtight container at room temperature.
4. Serve with yogurt, milk, or as a topping for smoothie bowls.

Nutritional Data: 220 calories | 25g carbs | 5g protein | 10g fat | 4g fiber | 12g sugar

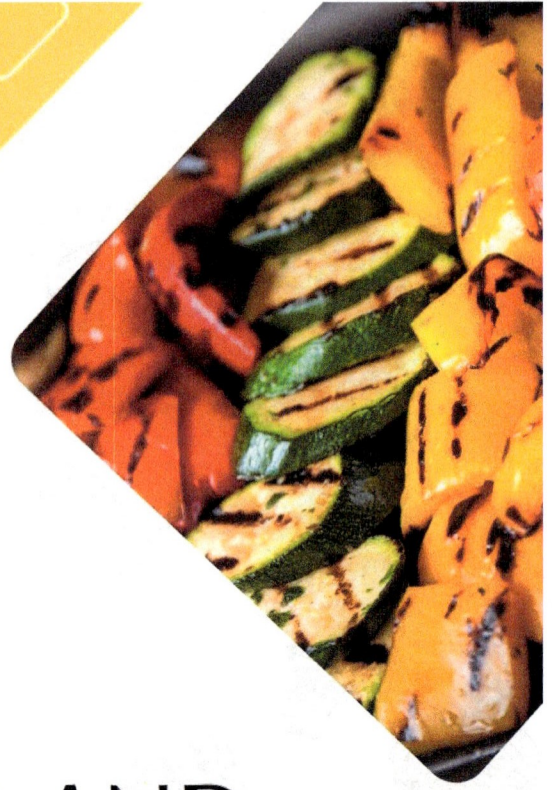

SIDE DISHES AND VEGETABLES

35. Parmesan Garlic Zucchini Slices

★★★★

🕐 10 Minuten   🍳🕐 15 Minuten   🍴 4 servings

INGREDIENTS

- 2 zucchinis, sliced into rounds
- 1/4 cup grated Parmesan cheese
- 2 cloves garlic, minced
- 2 tablespoons olive oil
- Salt and pepper to taste

INSTRUCTIONS

1. In a bowl, toss zucchini slices with grated Parmesan cheese, minced garlic, olive oil, salt, and pepper until evenly coated.
2. Preheat the air fryer to 375°F (190°C).
3. Place the seasoned zucchini slices in the air fryer basket in a single layer.
4. Air fry for 8-10 minutes until golden brown and crispy.
5. Serve hot as a delicious and nutritious side dish.

Nutritional Data: 120 calories | 6g carbs | 4g protein | 10g fat | 2g fiber | 2g sugar

36. Spicy Sweet Potato Wedges

★★★★★

🕐 15 Minuten   🍳🕐 20 Minuten   🍴 4 servings

INGREDIENTS

- 2 sweet potatoes, cut into wedges
- 2 tablespoons olive oil
- 1 teaspoon chili powder
- 1/2 teaspoon paprika
- 1/2 teaspoon garlic powder
- Salt and pepper to taste

INSTRUCTIONS

1. In a bowl, toss sweet potato wedges with olive oil, chili powder, paprika, garlic powder, salt, and pepper until evenly coated.
2. Preheat the air fryer to 400°F (200°C).
3. Place the seasoned sweet potato wedges in the air fryer basket in a single layer.
4. Air fry for 15-20 minutes until crispy on the outside and tender on the inside.
5. Serve hot as a flavorful side dish or snack.

Nutritional Data: 150 calories | 20g carbs | 2g protein | 7g fat | 3g fiber | 5g sugar

37.Crispy Brussels Sprout Chips

★★★★

🕐 10 Minuten   ♨🕐 15 Minuten   🍴 4 servings

INGREDIENTS

- 1 pound Brussels sprouts, trimmed and halved
- 2 tablespoons olive oil
- Salt and pepper to taste

INSTRUCTIONS

1. In a bowl, toss Brussels sprout halves with olive oil, salt, and pepper until evenly coated.
2. Preheat the air fryer to 375°F (190°C).
3. Place the seasoned Brussels sprout halves in the air fryer basket in a single layer.
4. Air fry for 10-15 minutes until crispy and golden brown.
5. Serve hot as a crunchy and nutritious snack or side dish.

Nutritional Data: 100 calories | 10g carbs | 5g protein | 6g fat | 4g fiber | 2g sugar

38.Italian Herb Tomatoes

★★★★★

🕐 5 Minuten   ♨🕐 10 Minuten   🍴 4 servings

INGREDIENTS

- 4 large tomatoes, halved
- 2 tablespoons olive oil
- 2 cloves garlic, minced
- 1 teaspoon dried Italian herbs (such as basil, oregano, thyme)
- Salt and pepper to taste

INSTRUCTIONS

1. Preheat the air fryer to 375°F (190°C).
2. In a bowl, toss tomato halves with olive oil, minced garlic, dried Italian herbs, salt, and pepper until evenly coated.
3. Place the seasoned tomato halves in the air fryer basket, cut side up.
4. Air fry for 8-10 minutes until tomatoes are softened and lightly browned.
5. Serve hot as a flavorful side dish or topping for salads and pasta dishes.

Nutritional Data: 80 calories | 6g carbs | 2g protein | 6g fat | 2g fiber | 4g sugar

39. Caramelized Balsamic Red Cabbage Steaks

★★★★

🕐 10 Minuten   ♨🕐 20 Minuten   🍴 4 servings

INSTRUCTIONS

1. Preheat the air fryer to 375°F (190°C).
2. In a bowl, whisk together olive oil, balsamic vinegar, honey or maple syrup, salt, and pepper.
3. Brush both sides of the red cabbage steaks with the balsamic mixture.
4. Place the cabbage steaks in the air fryer basket in a single layer.
5. Air fry for 15-20 minutes, flipping halfway through, until cabbage is caramelized and tender.
6. Serve hot as a sweet and tangy side dish.

INGREDIENTS

- 1 small red cabbage, sliced into steaks
- 2 tablespoons olive oil
- 2 tablespoons balsamic vinegar
- 1 tablespoon honey or maple syrup
- Salt and pepper to taste

Nutritional Data: 100 calories | 10g carbs | 2g protein | 6g fat | 3g fiber | 6g sugar

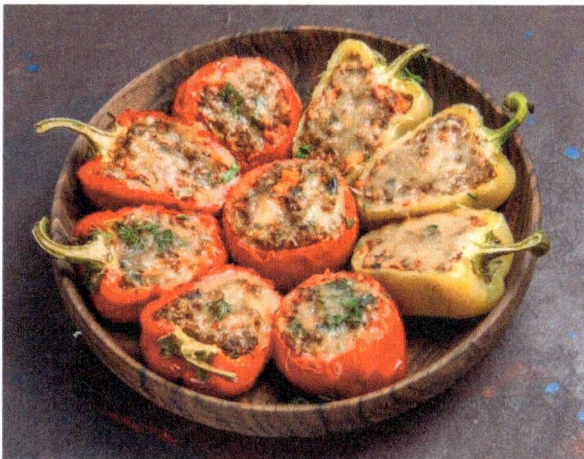

40. Roasted Peppers with Feta Filling

★★★★★

🕐 15 Minuten   ♨🕐 15 Minuten   🍴 4 servings

INSTRUCTIONS

1. Preheat the air fryer to 375°F (190°C).
2. In a bowl, mix together crumbled feta cheese, chopped fresh herbs, olive oil, salt, and pepper.
3. Fill each bell pepper half with the feta mixture.
4. Place the stuffed bell peppers in the air fryer basket.
5. Air fry for 12-15 minutes until peppers are softened and filling is golden brown.
6. Serve hot as a savory appetizer or side dish.

INGREDIENTS

- 2 large bell peppers (any color), halved and seeded
- 1/2 cup crumbled feta cheese
- 1/4 cup chopped fresh herbs (such as parsley, basil, chives)
- 2 tablespoons olive oil
- Salt and pepper to taste

Nutritional Data: 150 calories | 8g carbs | 5g protein | 10g fat | 2g fiber | 4g sugar

41. Turmeric Cauliflower Florets

★★★★

🕐 **10 Minuten**   ♨🕐 **15 Minuten**   🍴 **4 servings**

INGREDIENTS

- 1 head cauliflower, cut into florets
- 2 tablespoons olive oil
- 1 teaspoon ground turmeric
- 1/2 teaspoon ground cumin
- 1/2 teaspoon smoked paprika
- Salt and pepper to taste

INSTRUCTIONS

1. Preheat the air fryer to 375°F (190°C).
2. In a bowl, toss cauliflower florets with olive oil, ground turmeric, ground cumin, smoked paprika, salt, and pepper until evenly coated.
3. Place the seasoned cauliflower florets in the air fryer basket in a single layer.
4. Air fry for 12-15 minutes until cauliflower is tender and lightly browned.
5. Serve hot as a flavorful and nutritious side dish.

Nutritional Data: 90 calories | 10g carbs | 3g protein | 6g fat | 4g fiber | 4g sugar

42. Garlic Butter Mushrooms

★★★★★

🕐 **10 Minuten**   ♨🕐 **10 Minuten**   🍴 **4 servings**

INGREDIENTS

- 1 pound mushrooms, cleaned and quartered
- 2 tablespoons butter, melted
- 2 cloves garlic, minced
- 2 tablespoons chopped fresh parsley
- Salt and pepper to taste

INSTRUCTIONS

1. Preheat the air fryer to 375°F (190°C).
2. In a bowl, toss quartered mushrooms with melted butter, minced garlic, chopped fresh parsley, salt, and pepper until evenly coated.
3. Place the seasoned mushrooms in the air fryer basket.
4. Air fry for 8-10 minutes until mushrooms are tender and golden brown.
5. Serve hot as a delicious and savory side dish or topping for steaks and pasta.

Nutritional Data: 100 calories | 5g carbs | 4g protein | 8g fat | 2g fiber | 2g sugar

43. Asian Soy Glazed Eggplant

★★★★

🕐 **15 Minuten**　　🍳🕐 **15 Minuten**　　🍴 **4 servings**

INGREDIENTS

- 2 medium eggplants, sliced into rounds
- 1/4 cup soy sauce
- 2 tablespoons honey or maple syrup
- 1 tablespoon rice vinegar
- 1 teaspoon sesame oil
- 2 cloves garlic, minced
- 1 teaspoon grated ginger
- 1 green onion, chopped (for garnish)

INSTRUCTIONS

1. Preheat the air fryer to 375°F (190°C).
2. In a bowl, whisk together soy sauce, honey or maple syrup, rice vinegar, sesame oil, minced garlic, and grated ginger to make the glaze.
3. Brush both sides of the eggplant slices with the glaze.
4. Place the glazed eggplant slices in the air fryer basket in a single layer.
5. Air fry for 12-15 minutes until eggplant is tender and glazed.
6. Garnish with chopped green onions before serving.
7. Serve hot as a flavorful side dish or appetizer.

Nutritional Data: 120 calories | 15g carbs | 2g protein | 6g fat | 4g fiber | 10g sugar

44. Lemon Thyme Green Beans

★★★★★

🕐 **10 Minuten**　　🍳🕐 **10 Minuten**　　🍴 **4 servings**

INGREDIENTS

- 1 pound green beans, trimmed
- 2 tablespoons olive oil
- Zest and juice of 1 lemon
- 2 teaspoons fresh thyme leaves
- Salt and pepper to taste

INSTRUCTIONS

1. Preheat the air fryer to 375°F (190°C).
2. In a bowl, toss trimmed green beans with olive oil, lemon zest, lemon juice, fresh thyme leaves, salt, and pepper until evenly coated.
3. Place the seasoned green beans in the air fryer basket.
4. Air fry for 8-10 minutes until green beans are tender and lightly charred.
5. Serve hot as a vibrant and flavorful side dish.

Nutritional Data: 80 calories | 10g carbs | 2g protein | 4g fat | 4g fiber | 4g sugar

45. Smoked Paprika and Potato Wedges

★★★★

🕐 15 Minuten   🍳🕐 25 Minuten   🍴 4 servings

INGREDIENTS

- 4 medium potatoes, cut into wedges
- 2 tablespoons olive oil
- 1 teaspoon smoked paprika
- 1/2 teaspoon garlic powder
- 1/2 teaspoon onion powder
- Salt and pepper to taste

INSTRUCTIONS

1. Preheat the air fryer to 375°F (190°C).
2. In a bowl, toss potato wedges with olive oil, smoked paprika, garlic powder, onion powder, salt, and pepper until evenly coated.
3. Place the seasoned potato wedges in the air fryer basket in a single layer.
4. Air fry for 20-25 minutes, flipping halfway through, until crispy and golden brown.
5. Serve hot as a delicious and satisfying side dish or snack.

Nutritional Data: 150 calories | 20g carbs | 2g protein | 7g fat | 3g fiber | 2g sugar

46. Mediterranean Vegetable Mix

★★★★

🕐 15 Minuten   🍳🕐 20 Minuten   🍴 4 servings

INGREDIENTS

- 1 large bell pepper (any color), sliced
- 1 large zucchini, sliced
- 1 large yellow squash, sliced
- 1 red onion, sliced
- 2 tablespoons olive oil
- 2 teaspoons dried Italian herbs (such as basil, oregano, thyme)
- Salt and pepper to taste

INSTRUCTIONS

1. Preheat the air fryer to 375°F (190°C).
2. In a bowl, toss sliced bell pepper, zucchini, yellow squash, and red onion with olive oil, dried Italian herbs, salt, and pepper until evenly coated.
3. Place the seasoned vegetables in the air fryer basket.
4. Air fry for 12-15 minutes, stirring halfway through, until vegetables are tender and lightly browned.
5. Serve hot as a flavorful and colorful side dish.

Nutritional Data: 120 calories | 10g carbs | 2g protein | 8g fat | 3g fiber | 6g sugar

FISH AND SEAFOOD

47. Crispy Salmon Fillets with Dill-Mustard Crust

★★★★★

🕐 **10 Minuten**   🍳🕐 **15 Minuten**   🍴 **2 servings**

INGREDIENTS

- 2 salmon fillets (about 6 oz each)
- 2 tablespoons Dijon mustard
- 2 tablespoons chopped fresh dill
- 1/4 cup breadcrumbs
- 2 tablespoons grated Parmesan cheese
- Salt and pepper to taste

INSTRUCTIONS

1. Preheat the air fryer to 375°F (190°C).
2. Season the salmon fillets with salt and pepper.
3. In a small bowl, mix together Dijon mustard and chopped fresh dill.
4. In another bowl, combine breadcrumbs and grated Parmesan cheese.
5. Spread the mustard mixture evenly on top of each salmon fillet.
6. Press the breadcrumb mixture onto the mustard-coated salmon fillets to form a crust.
7. Place the salmon fillets in the air fryer basket.
8. Air fry for 12-15 minutes until the salmon is cooked through and the crust is golden and crispy.
9. Serve hot with your favorite side dishes.

Nutritional Data: 320 calories | 10g carbs | 40g protein | 14g fat | 2g fiber | 2g sugar

48. Spicy Shrimp with Garlic-Lime Marinade

★★★★

🕐 **10 Minuten**   🍳🕐 **6 Minuten**   🍴 **2 servings**

INGREDIENTS

- 1/2 pound large shrimp, peeled and deveined
- 2 cloves garlic, minced
- 2 tablespoons olive oil
- Juice of 1 lime
- 1 teaspoon chili powder
- 1/2 teaspoon paprika
- Salt and pepper to taste

INSTRUCTIONS

1. In a bowl, mix together minced garlic, olive oil, lime juice, chili powder, paprika, salt, and pepper to make the marinade.
2. Add the shrimp to the marinade and toss to coat evenly. Let marinate for 10-15 minutes.
3. Preheat the air fryer to 400°F (200°C).
4. Place the marinated shrimp in the air fryer basket in a single layer.
5. Air fry for 5-6 minutes until shrimp are pink and cooked through.
6. Serve hot as an appetizer or with rice and vegetables.

Nutritional Data: 180 calories | 3g carbs | 20g protein | 10g fat | 0g fiber | 0g sugar

49. Sweet and Spicy Tuna Steaks

★★★★★

🕐 **10 Minuten** ♨🕐 **8 Minuten** 🍴 **2 servings**

INGREDIENTS

- 2 tuna steaks (about 6 oz each)
- 2 tablespoons soy sauce
- 2 tablespoons honey
- 1 tablespoon sriracha sauce
- 1 tablespoon olive oil
- 2 cloves garlic, minced
- Salt and pepper to taste

INSTRUCTIONS

1. In a bowl, whisk together soy sauce, honey, sriracha sauce, olive oil, minced garlic, salt, and pepper to make the marinade.
2. Place the tuna steaks in a shallow dish and pour the marinade over them. Marinate for 15-30 minutes.
3. Preheat the air fryer to 400°F (200°C).
4. Remove the tuna steaks from the marinade and pat dry with paper towels.
5. Place the tuna steaks in the air fryer basket.
6. Air fry for 7-8 minutes for medium-rare, or longer if desired.
7. Serve hot with steamed rice and your favorite vegetables.

Nutritional Data: 280 calories | 15g carbs | 30g protein | 12g fat | 0g fiber | 10g sugar

50. Lemon Caper Cod

★★★★

🕐 **10 Minuten** ♨🕐 **10 Minuten** 🍴 **2 servings**

INGREDIENTS

- 2 cod fillets (about 6 oz each)
- 2 tablespoons olive oil
- 2 tablespoons lemon juice
- 2 tablespoons capers, drained
- 2 cloves garlic, minced
- 1 tablespoon chopped fresh parsley
- Salt and pepper to taste

INSTRUCTIONS

1. Preheat the air fryer to 375°F (190°C).
2. In a small bowl, mix together olive oil, lemon juice, capers, minced garlic, chopped fresh parsley, salt, and pepper.
3. Place the cod fillets in the air fryer basket.
4. Spoon the lemon caper mixture over the cod fillets.
5. Air fry for 8-10 minutes until the cod is cooked through and flakes easily with a fork.
6. Serve hot with steamed vegetables or a side salad.

Nutritional Data: 250 calories | 2g carbs | 30g protein | 14g fat | 1g fiber | 0g sugar

51. Asian Tilapia Packets with Vegetables

★★★★★

🕐 **15 Minuten**   🍳🕐 **15 Minuten**   🍴 **2 servings**

INGREDIENTS

- 2 tilapia fillets (about 6 oz each)
- 1 cup mixed vegetables (such as bell peppers, snap peas, carrots)
- 2 tablespoons soy sauce
- 1 tablespoon hoisin sauce
- 1 tablespoon rice vinegar
- 1 teaspoon sesame oil
- 2 cloves garlic, minced
- 1 teaspoon grated ginger
- Salt and pepper to taste

INSTRUCTIONS

1. Preheat the air fryer to 375°F (190°C).
2. In a bowl, mix together soy sauce, hoisin sauce, rice vinegar, sesame oil, minced garlic, grated ginger, salt, and pepper.
3. Place each tilapia fillet on a piece of parchment paper or aluminum foil.
4. Divide the mixed vegetables between the tilapia packets.
5. Drizzle the soy sauce mixture over the tilapia and vegetables.
6. Fold the parchment paper or aluminum foil to seal the packets.
7. Place the packets in the air fryer basket.
8. Air fry for 12-15 minutes until the tilapia is cooked through and the vegetables are tender.
9. Serve hot with rice or noodles.

Nutritional Data: 200 calories | 10g carbs | 25g protein | 8g fat | 3g fiber | 4g sugar

52. Honey Sesame Shrimp Skewers

★★★★★

🕐 **10 Minuten**   🍳🕐 **6 Minuten**   🍴 **2 servings**

INGREDIENTS

- 1/2 pound large shrimp, peeled and deveined
- 2 tablespoons honey
- 1 tablespoon soy sauce
- 1 tablespoon sesame oil
- 1 teaspoon grated ginger
- 1 clove garlic, minced
- 1 tablespoon sesame seeds
- Salt and pepper to taste

INSTRUCTIONS

1. In a bowl, whisk together honey, soy sauce, sesame oil, grated ginger, minced garlic, sesame seeds, salt, and pepper to make the marinade.
2. Add the shrimp to the marinade and toss to coat evenly. Let marinate for 10-15 minutes.
3. Preheat the air fryer to 400°F (200°C).
4. Thread the marinated shrimp onto skewers.
5. Place the shrimp skewers in the air fryer basket.
6. Air fry for 5-6 minutes until shrimp are pink and cooked through.
7. Serve hot with rice or as an appetizer with dipping sauce.

Nutritional Data: 180 calories | 10g carbs | 20g protein | 7g fat | 1g fiber | 8g sugar

53. Herb and Garlic Scampi

★★★★★

🕐 10Minuten   ♨🕐 10 Minuten   🍴 2 servings

INGREDIENTS

- 1/2 pound large shrimp, peeled and deveined
- 2 tablespoons butter
- 2 cloves garlic, minced
- 2 tablespoons chopped fresh parsley
- 1 tablespoon lemon juice
- Salt and pepper to taste

INSTRUCTIONS

1. Preheat the air fryer to 375°F (190°C).
2. In a small bowl, mix together melted butter, minced garlic, chopped fresh parsley, lemon juice, salt, and pepper.
3. Place the shrimp in the air fryer basket.
4. Pour the herb and garlic mixture over the shrimp.
5. Air fry for 8-10 minutes until the shrimp are pink and cooked through.
6. Serve hot with pasta or crusty bread.

Nutritional Data: 220 calories | 2g carbs | 20g protein | 15g fat | 0g fiber | 0g sugar

54. Breaded Plaice Fillets with Tartar Sauce

★★★★★

🕐 15 Minuten   ♨🕐 10 Minuten   🍴 4 servings

INSTRUCTIONS

1. Preheat the air fryer to 375°F (190°C).
2. In a shallow dish, mix together breadcrumbs, grated Parmesan cheese, dried dill, lemon zest, salt, and pepper.
3. Dip each plaice fillet into the beaten egg, then dredge in the breadcrumb mixture, pressing gently to adhere.
4. Place the breaded plaice fillets in the air fryer basket.
5. Air fry for 8-10 minutes until the fish is cooked through and the coating is golden and crispy.
6. Serve hot with tartar sauce and lemon wedges.

INGREDIENTS

- 2 plaice fillets (about 6 oz each)
- 1/2 cup breadcrumbs
- 2 tablespoons grated Parmesan cheese
- 1 teaspoon dried dill
- 1 teaspoon lemon zest
- Salt and pepper to taste
- 1 egg, beaten
- Tartar sauce for serving

Nutritional Data: 280 calories | 20g carbs | 25g protein | 12g fat | 1g fiber | 1g sugar

55. Curry Salmon Cubes

★★★★

🕐 10 Minuten   ♨🕐 10 Minuten   🍴 2 servings

INGREDIENTS

- 2 salmon fillets (about 6 oz each), cut into cubes
- 2 tablespoons olive oil
- 2 teaspoons curry powder
- 1 teaspoon ground cumin
- 1/2 teaspoon paprika
- Salt and pepper to taste

INSTRUCTIONS

1. Preheat the air fryer to 375°F (190°C).
2. In a bowl, mix together olive oil, curry powder, ground cumin, paprika, salt, and pepper.
3. Add the salmon cubes to the spice mixture and toss to coat evenly.
4. Place the seasoned salmon cubes in the air fryer basket.
5. Air fry for 8-10 minutes until salmon is cooked through and lightly browned.
6. Serve hot with rice or naan bread.

Nutritional Data: 320 calories | 3g carbs | 30g protein | 20g fat | 1g fiber | 0g sugar

56. Zesty Lemon Pepper Shrimp

★★★★★

🕐 10 Minuten   ♨🕐 6 Minuten   🍴 2 servings

INGREDIENTS

- 1/2 pound large shrimp, peeled and deveined
- 2 tablespoons olive oil
- 1 teaspoon lemon zest
- 1 tablespoon lemon juice
- 1 teaspoon freshly ground black pepper
- Salt to taste

INSTRUCTIONS

1. In a bowl, mix together olive oil, lemon zest, lemon juice, freshly ground black pepper, and salt.
2. Add the shrimp to the lemon pepper mixture and toss to coat evenly.
3. Preheat the air fryer to 400°F (200°C).
4. Place the marinated shrimp in the air fryer basket.
5. Air fry for 5-6 minutes until shrimp are pink and cooked through.
6. Serve hot as an appetizer or with pasta or rice.

Nutritional Data: 200 calories | 1g carbs | 20g protein | 14g fat | 0g fiber | 0g sugar

57.KokosnCoconut Curry Musselsuss-Curry-Muscheln

★ ★ ★ ★

🕐 **15Minuten**   ♨🕐 **10 Minuten**   🍴 **4 servings**

INSTRUCTIONS

1. Preheat the air fryer to 375°F (190°C).
2. In a bowl, mix together olive oil, minced garlic, and red curry paste.
3. Add the cleaned mussels to the curry mixture and toss to coat evenly.
4. Place the mussels in the air fryer basket.
5. Pour coconut milk over the mussels.
6. Air fry for 6-8 minutes until mussels are cooked through and shells have opened.
7. Discard any unopened mussels before serving.
8. Garnish with chopped fresh cilantro.

Serve hot with crusty bread for dipping.

INGREDIENTS

- 1 pound mussels, cleaned and debearded
- 1 tablespoon olive oil
- 2 cloves garlic, minced
- 1 tablespoon red curry paste
- 1 cup coconut milk
- 2 tablespoons chopped fresh cilantro
- Salt and pepper to taste

Nutritional Data: 280 calories | 8g carbs | 15g protein | 20g fat | 1g fiber | 2g sugar

58.Spicy Squid with Aioli Dip

★ ★ ★ ★ ★

🕐 **15 Minuten**   ♨🕐 **10 Minuten**   🍴 **2 servings**

INSTRUCTIONS

1. Preheat the air fryer to 375°F (190°C).
2. In a shallow dish, mix together breadcrumbs, grated Parmesan cheese, paprika, cayenne pepper, salt, and pepper.
3. Dip each squid ring into the breadcrumb mixture, pressing gently to coat evenly.
4. Place the breaded squid rings in the air fryer basket.
5. Air fry for 8-10 minutes until squid is golden and crispy.
6. Serve hot with aioli dip and lemon wedges.

INGREDIENTS

- 1/2 pound squid, cleaned and sliced into rings
- 1/4 cup breadcrumbs
- 1/4 cup grated Parmesan cheese
- 1 teaspoon paprika
- 1/2 teaspoon cayenne pepper
- Salt and pepper to taste
- Aioli dip for serving

Nutritional Data: 220 calories | 15g carbs | 20g protein | 10g fat | 1g fiber | 1g sugar

59. Creole Catfish with Remoulade

★★★★★

🕐 **15 Minuten**   ♨🕐 **10 Minuten**   🍴 **2 servings**

INGREDIENTS

- 2 catfish fillets (about 6 oz each)
- 1/2 cup breadcrumbs
- 2 tablespoons grated Parmesan cheese
- 1 teaspoon Creole seasoning
- 1 teaspoon dried thyme
- Salt and pepper to taste
- Remoulade sauce for serving

INSTRUCTIONS

1. Preheat the air fryer to 375°F (190°C).
2. In a shallow dish, mix together breadcrumbs, grated Parmesan cheese, Creole seasoning, dried thyme, salt, and pepper.
3. Dip each catfish fillet into the breadcrumb mixture, pressing gently to coat evenly.
4. Place the breaded catfish fillets in the air fryer basket.
5. Air fry for 8-10 minutes until catfish is cooked through and coating is golden and crispy.
6. Serve hot with remoulade sauce and lemon wedges.

Nutritional Data: 280 calories | 20g carbs | 25g protein | 12g fat | 1g fiber | 1g sugar

60. Provencal Prawns with Garlic and Herbs

★★★★

🕐 **10 Minuten**   ♨🕐 **6 Minuten**   🍴 **2 servings**

INGREDIENTS

- 1/2 pound large prawns, peeled and deveined
- 2 tablespoons olive oil
- 2 cloves garlic, minced
- 2 tablespoons chopped fresh parsley
- 1 tablespoon chopped fresh basil
- 1 tablespoon chopped fresh thyme
- Salt and pepper to taste

INSTRUCTIONS

1. In a bowl, mix together olive oil, minced garlic, chopped fresh parsley, chopped fresh basil, chopped fresh thyme, salt, and pepper.
2. Add the prawns to the herb and garlic mixture and toss to coat evenly.
3. Preheat the air fryer to 400°F (200°C).
4. Place the marinated prawns in the air fryer basket.
5. Air fry for 5-6 minutes until prawns are pink and cooked through.
6. Serve hot with crusty bread or over pasta.

Nutritional Data: 180 calories | 2g carbs | 20g protein | 10g fat | 0g fiber | 0g sugar

61. Smoky Trout with Cedar Wood Aroma

★★★★★

🕐 **10 Minuten**   ♨🕐 **12 Minuten**   🍴 **2 servings**

INSTRUCTIONS

1. Preheat the air fryer to 375°F (190°C).
2. In a bowl, mix together olive oil, smoked paprika, garlic powder, onion powder, salt, and pepper.
3. Rub the spice mixture evenly over both sides of the trout fillets.
4. Place the trout fillets in the air fryer basket.
5. Air fry for 10-12 minutes until trout is cooked through and flakes easily with a fork.
6. Serve hot with lemon wedges.

INGREDIENTS

- 2 trout fillets (about 6 oz each)
- 2 tablespoons olive oil
- 1 teaspoon smoked paprika
- 1/2 teaspoon garlic powder
- 1/2 teaspoon onion powder
- Salt and pepper to taste

Nutritional Data: 280 calories | 0g carbs | 30g protein | 16g fat | 0g fiber | 0g sugar

62. Cod Fillet with Crispy Breading and Lemon Dill Dip

★★★★

🕐 **10 Minuten**   ♨🕐 **15 Minuten**   🍴 **2 servings**

INSTRUCTIONS

1. Preheat the air fryer to 375°F (190°C).
2. In a shallow dish, mix together breadcrumbs, grated Parmesan cheese, dried dill, garlic powder, onion powder, salt, and pepper.
3. Pat the cod fillets dry with paper towels.
4. Dip each cod fillet into the breadcrumb mixture, pressing gently to coat evenly.
5. Place the breaded cod fillets in the air fryer basket.
6. Air fry for 12-15 minutes until the cod is cooked through and the coating is golden and crispy.
7. Serve hot with lemon wedges and lemon dill dip.

INGREDIENTS

- 2 cod fillets (about 6 oz each)
- 1/2 cup breadcrumbs
- 2 tablespoons grated Parmesan cheese
- 1 teaspoon dried dill
- 1/2 teaspoon garlic powder
- 1/2 teaspoon onion powder
- Salt and pepper to taste
- Lemon wedges for serving

Nutritional Data: 300 calories | 20g carbs | 30g protein | 12g fat | 1g fiber | 1g sugar

63. Deep Fryer Style Seafood Paella

★★★★★

🕐 **20 Minuten** 〰️🕐 **25 Minuten** 🍴 **4 servings**

INGREDIENTS

- 1 cup arborio rice
- 1/2 pound shrimp, peeled and deveined
- 1/2 pound mussels, cleaned and debearded
- 1/2 pound calamari rings
- 1/2 cup diced chorizo
- 1 onion, chopped
- 2 cloves garlic, minced
- 1 red bell pepper, diced
- 1 tomato, diced
- 2 cups chicken broth
- 1 teaspoon smoked paprika
- 1/2 teaspoon saffron threads
- Salt and pepper to taste
- Lemon wedges for serving

INSTRUCTIONS

1. In a bowl, soak saffron threads in 2 tablespoons of warm water for 10 minutes.
2. Preheat the air fryer to 375°F (190°C).
3. In a large skillet, heat olive oil over medium heat. Add chopped onion, minced garlic, diced chorizo, and diced red bell pepper. Cook until vegetables are softened and chorizo is browned.
4. Stir in arborio rice, diced tomato, smoked paprika, soaked saffron threads with water, salt, and pepper. Cook for 1-2 minutes.
5. Transfer the rice mixture to the air fryer basket. Pour chicken broth over the rice mixture.
6. Cook in the air fryer for 20-25 minutes until the rice is cooked through and the liquid is absorbed.
7. Arrange shrimp, mussels, and calamari rings on top of the rice mixture.
8. Continue to cook in the air fryer for an additional 5-7 minutes until the seafood is cooked through.
9. Serve hot with lemon wedges.

Nutritional Data: 380 calories | 40g carbs | 30g protein | 12g fat | 2g fiber | 2g sugar

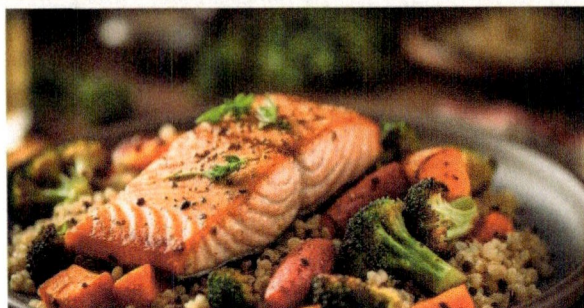

64. Teriyaki Salmon with Sesame Vegetables

★★★★

🕐 **15 Minuten** 〰️🕐 **12 Minuten** 🍴 **4 servings**

INGREDIENTS

- 2 salmon fillets (about 6 oz each)
- 1/4 cup teriyaki sauce
- 1 tablespoon sesame oil
- 2 tablespoons soy sauce
- 1 tablespoon rice vinegar
- 1 tablespoon honey
- 2 cloves garlic, minced
- 1 teaspoon grated ginger
- 1 cup mixed vegetables (such as bell peppers, snap peas, carrots)
- 1 tablespoon sesame seeds
- Green onions, sliced, for garnish

INSTRUCTIONS

1. In a bowl, whisk together teriyaki sauce, sesame oil, soy sauce, rice vinegar, honey, minced garlic, and grated ginger to make the marinade.
2. Add the salmon fillets to the marinade and let marinate for 15-30 minutes.
3. Preheat the air fryer to 375°F (190°C).
4. In a separate bowl, toss mixed vegetables with a little bit of olive oil, salt, and pepper.
5. Place the marinated salmon fillets and mixed vegetables in the air fryer basket.
6. Air fry for 10-12 minutes until salmon is cooked through and vegetables are tender.
7. Garnish with sesame seeds and sliced green onions.
8. Serve hot with steamed rice.

Nutritional Data: 320 calories | 20g carbs | 30g protein | 14g fat | 2g fiber | 12g sugar

65. Hot and Sweet Mango Prawns

★★★★★

🕐 **15 Minuten**   ♨🕐 **6 Minuten**   🍴 **2 servings**

INGREDIENTS

- 1/2 pound large prawns, peeled and deveined
- 1 ripe mango, peeled and diced
- 2 tablespoons honey
- 1 tablespoon soy sauce
- 1 tablespoon sriracha sauce
- 1 tablespoon lime juice
- 1 clove garlic, minced
- Salt and pepper to taste

INSTRUCTIONS

1. In a bowl, mix together diced mango, honey, soy sauce, sriracha sauce, lime juice, minced garlic, salt, and pepper.
2. Add the prawns to the mango mixture and toss to coat evenly. Let marinate for 10-15 minutes.
3. Preheat the air fryer to 400°F (200°C).
4. Place the marinated prawns in the air fryer basket.
5. Air fry for 5-6 minutes until prawns are pink and cooked through.
6. Serve hot as an appetizer or with rice.

Nutritional Data: 200 calories | 15g carbs | 20g protein | 8g fat | 1g fiber | 12g sugar

66. Pesto Shrimp with Cherry Tomatoes

★★★★

🕐 **15 Minuten**   ♨🕐 **6 Minuten**   🍴 **2 servings**

INGREDIENTS

- 1/2 pound large shrimp, peeled and deveined
- 1/4 cup prepared pesto sauce
- 1 cup cherry tomatoes, halved
- 2 tablespoons grated Parmesan cheese
- Salt and pepper to taste

INSTRUCTIONS

1. In a bowl, toss shrimp with prepared pesto sauce until evenly coated.
2. Preheat the air fryer to 400°F (200°C).
3. Place the shrimp in the air fryer basket.
4. Add halved cherry tomatoes to the air fryer basket.
5. Air fry for 5-6 minutes until shrimp are pink and cooked through.
6. Sprinkle grated Parmesan cheese over the shrimp and tomatoes.
7. Serve hot with crusty bread or over pasta.

Nutritional Data: 220 calories | 5g carbs | 20g protein | 14g fat | 1g fiber | 3g sugar

67. Quick Fish Tacos with Cabbage Slaw

★★★★

🕐 20 Minuten   ♨🕐 12 Minuten   🍴 4 servings

INGREDIENTS

- 2 cod fillets (about 6 oz each)
- 1 tablespoon olive oil
- 1 teaspoon chili powder
- 1/2 teaspoon ground cumin
- 1/2 teaspoon garlic powder
- Salt and pepper to taste
- 4 small flour tortillas
- 1 cup shredded cabbage
- 1/4 cup chopped fresh cilantro
- 1/4 cup sour cream
- 1 lime, cut into wedges

INSTRUCTIONS

1. Preheat the air fryer to 375°F (190°C).
2. In a small bowl, mix together olive oil, chili powder, ground cumin, garlic powder, salt, and pepper.
3. Rub the spice mixture evenly over both sides of the cod fillets.
4. Place the cod fillets in the air fryer basket.
5. Air fry for 6-8 minutes until cod is cooked through and flakes easily with a fork.
6. Meanwhile, warm the flour tortillas in the air fryer for 1-2 minutes.
7. In a bowl, toss shredded cabbage with chopped fresh cilantro and a squeeze of lime juice.
8. Flake the cooked cod and divide it among the warmed tortillas.
9. Top with cabbage slaw and a dollop of sour cream.
10. Serve hot with lime wedges.

Nutritional Data: 320 calories | 25g carbs | 25g protein | 14g fat | 2g fiber | 2g sugar

68. Lemon Basil Halibut

★★★★★

🕐 10 Minuten   ♨🕐 12 Minuten   🍴 2 servings

INGREDIENTS

- 2 halibut fillets (about 6 oz each)
- 2 tablespoons olive oil
- Zest of 1 lemon
- Juice of 1 lemon
- 2 cloves garlic, minced
- 2 tablespoons chopped fresh basil
- Salt and pepper to taste

INSTRUCTIONS

1. Preheat the air fryer to 375°F (190°C).
2. In a small bowl, mix together olive oil, lemon zest, lemon juice, minced garlic, chopped fresh basil, salt, and pepper.
3. Place the halibut fillets in the air fryer basket.
4. Spoon the lemon basil mixture over the halibut fillets.
5. Air fry for 10-12 minutes until halibut is cooked through and flakes easily with a fork.
6. Serve hot with steamed vegetables or a side salad.

Nutritional Data: 250 calories | 0g carbs | 30g protein | 14g fat | 0g fiber | 0g sugar

69. Nourishing Crispy Calamari Rings

★★★★

⏱ 15 Minuten   🍳⏱ 8 Minuten   🍴 4 servings

INGREDIENTS

- 1/2 pound calamari rings
- 1/2 cup all-purpose flour
- 2 eggs, beaten
- 1 cup breadcrumbs
- 1/4 cup grated Parmesan cheese
- 1 teaspoon dried oregano
- 1 teaspoon smoked paprika
- Salt and pepper to taste
- Marinara sauce for serving

INSTRUCTIONS

1. Preheat the air fryer to 375°F (190°C).
2. Place flour, beaten eggs, and breadcrumbs in separate shallow dishes.
3. In a bowl, mix together breadcrumbs, grated Parmesan cheese, dried oregano, smoked paprika, salt, and pepper.
4. Dip each calamari ring into the flour, then the beaten eggs, and finally the breadcrumb mixture, pressing gently to coat evenly.
5. Place the breaded calamari rings in the air fryer basket.
6. Air fry for 8-10 minutes until calamari is golden and crispy.
7. Serve hot with marinara sauce for dipping.

Nutritional Data: 300 calories | 25g carbs | 20g protein | 14g fat | 1g fiber | 1g sugar

70. Mediterranean Sea Bream with Olives and Tomatoes

★★★★★

⏱ 20 Minuten   🍳⏱ 15 Minuten   🍴 4 servings

INGREDIENTS

- 2 sea bream fillets (about 6 oz each)
- 1/2 cup cherry tomatoes, halved
- 1/4 cup pitted Kalamata olives, halved
- 2 cloves garlic, minced
- 2 tablespoons olive oil
- 1 tablespoon chopped fresh parsley
- 1 tablespoon chopped fresh basil
- Salt and pepper to taste

INSTRUCTIONS

1. Preheat the air fryer to 375°F (190°C).
2. In a bowl, mix together cherry tomatoes, Kalamata olives, minced garlic, olive oil, chopped fresh parsley, chopped fresh basil, salt, and pepper.
3. Place the sea bream fillets in the air fryer basket.
4. Spoon the tomato and olive mixture over the sea bream fillets.
5. Air fry for 12-15 minutes until sea bream is cooked through and flakes easily with a fork.
6. Serve hot with crusty bread or over couscous.

Nutritional Data: 280 calories | 5g carbs | 25g protein | 18g fat | 1g fiber | 2g sugar

MEAT

71. Breaded Pork Schnitzel

★★★★★

🕐 15 Minuten   ♨🕐 12 Minuten   🍴 2 servings

INGREDIENTS

- 2 pork schnitzels
- 1/2 cup all-purpose flour
- 2 eggs, beaten
- 1 cup breadcrumbs
- Salt and pepper to taste
- Lemon wedges for serving

INSTRUCTIONS

1. Season the pork schnitzels with salt and pepper.
2. Set up three shallow dishes: one with flour, one with beaten eggs, and one with breadcrumbs.
3. Dredge each schnitzel in the flour, then dip into the beaten eggs, and coat with breadcrumbs, pressing gently to adhere.
4. Preheat the air fryer to 375°F (190°C).
5. Place the breaded schnitzels in the air fryer basket in a single layer.
6. Air fry for 6 minutes, then flip the schnitzels and air fry for an additional 6 minutes until golden and crispy.
7. Serve hot with lemon wedges.

Nutritional Data: 380 calories | 30g carbs | 25g protein | 18g fat | 2g fiber | 1g sugar

72. Rosemary Lamb Chops

★★★★

🕐 10 Minuten   ♨🕐 10 Minuten   🍴 2 servings

INGREDIENTS

- 4 lamb chops
- 2 tablespoons olive oil
- 2 cloves garlic, minced
- 2 sprigs fresh rosemary, chopped
- Salt and pepper to taste

INSTRUCTIONS

1. In a bowl, mix together olive oil, minced garlic, chopped rosemary, salt, and pepper.
2. Rub the mixture over both sides of the lamb chops, ensuring they are evenly coated.
3. Preheat the air fryer to 400°F (200°C).
4. Place the lamb chops in the air fryer basket.
5. Air fry for 10 minutes, flipping halfway through, until lamb chops reach desired doneness.
6. Serve hot with your favorite side dishes.

Nutritional Data: 450 calories | 0g carbs | 30g protein | 35g fat | 0g fiber | 0g sugar

73. Teriyaki Beef Skewers

★★★★★

🕐 20 Minuten   ♨🕐 10Minuten   🍴 2 servings

INGREDIENTS

- 8 oz beef sirloin, cut into cubes
- 1/4 cup teriyaki sauce
- 1 tablespoon soy sauce
- 1 tablespoon honey
- 1 clove garlic, minced
- 1 teaspoon grated ginger
- Wooden skewers, soaked in water

INSTRUCTIONS

1. In a bowl, mix together teriyaki sauce, soy sauce, honey, minced garlic, and grated ginger.
2. Add the beef cubes to the marinade and let marinate for at least 15 minutes.
3. Preheat the air fryer to 400°F (200°C).
4. Thread the marinated beef cubes onto the soaked wooden skewers.
5. Place the skewers in the air fryer basket.
6. Air fry for 8-10 minutes, turning halfway through, until beef is cooked to your liking.
7. Serve hot with steamed rice and vegetables.

Nutritional Data: 320 calories | 15g carbs | 25g protein | 18g fat | 1g fiber | 12g sugar

74. Pulled Pork Burger

★★★★★

🕐 15 Minuten   ♨🕐 25 Minuten   🍴 2 servings

INGREDIENTS

- 8 oz pulled pork
- 2 burger buns
- 1/2 cup barbecue sauce
- 1/2 cup coleslaw
- Pickles, lettuce, and tomato slices for topping

INSTRUCTIONS

1. Preheat the air fryer to 375°F (190°C).
2. Spread barbecue sauce on both sides of the pulled pork.
3. Place the pulled pork in the air fryer basket.
4. Air fry for 10-12 minutes, stirring occasionally, until heated through.
5. Toast the burger buns in the air fryer for 2-3 minutes.
6. Assemble the burgers by placing pulled pork on the bottom bun, topping with coleslaw, pickles, lettuce, and tomato slices.
7. Serve hot with your favorite side dishes.

Nutritional Data: 450 calories | 40g carbs | 20g protein | 25g fat | 3g fiber | 15g sugar

75. Herb Butter Chicken Breast

★★★★★

🕐 10 Minuten   🍳🕐 20 Minuten   🍴 2 servings

INGREDIENTS

- 2 chicken breasts
- 2 tablespoons butter, melted
- 2 cloves garlic, minced
- 1 teaspoon dried thyme
- 1 teaspoon dried rosemary
- Salt and pepper to taste

INSTRUCTIONS

1. In a bowl, mix together melted butter, minced garlic, dried thyme, dried rosemary, salt, and pepper.
2. Rub the herb butter mixture over both sides of the chicken breasts.
3. Preheat the air fryer to 375°F (190°C).
4. Place the chicken breasts in the air fryer basket.
5. Air fry for 18-20 minutes, flipping halfway through, until chicken is cooked through and juices run clear.
6. Serve hot with your favorite side dishes.

Nutritional Data: 320 calories | og carbs | 30g protein | 20g fat | og fiber | og sugar

76. Chili Lime Pork Strips

★★★★★

🕐 15 Minuten   🍳🕐 12 Minuten   🍴 2 servings

INGREDIENTS

- 8 oz pork loin, thinly sliced
- 2 tablespoons olive oil
- Zest and juice of 1 lime
- 1 tablespoon chili powder
- 1 teaspoon garlic powder
- 1 teaspoon paprika
- Salt and pepper to taste

INSTRUCTIONS

1. In a bowl, mix together olive oil, lime zest, lime juice, chili powder, garlic powder, paprika, salt, and pepper.
2. Add the pork strips to the marinade and let marinate for at least 10 minutes.
3. Preheat the air fryer to 400°F (200°C).
4. Place the marinated pork strips in the air fryer basket.
5. Air fry for 10-12 minutes, shaking the basket halfway through, until pork is cooked through and slightly charred.
6. Serve hot with rice, beans, or tortillas.

Nutritional Data: 300 calories | 2g carbs | 25g protein | 22g fat | 1g fiber | og sugar

77. Stuffed Peppers with Minced Meat and Rice

⭐⭐⭐⭐⭐

🕐 **25 Minuten**   🍳🕐 **20Minuten**   🍴 **4 servings**

INGREDIENTS

- 4 bell peppers
- 1/2 pound ground beef or turkey
- 1/2 cup cooked rice
- 1/2 cup diced tomatoes
- 1/4 cup diced onion
- 1/4 cup shredded cheese
- 1 teaspoon Italian seasoning
- Salt and pepper to taste

INSTRUCTIONS

1. Preheat the air fryer to 375°F (190°C).
2. Cut the tops off the bell peppers and remove the seeds and membranes.
3. In a bowl, mix together ground beef or turkey, cooked rice, diced tomatoes, diced onion, shredded cheese, Italian seasoning, salt, and pepper.
4. Stuff the bell peppers with the meat and rice mixture.
5. Place the stuffed peppers in the air fryer basket.
6. Air fry for 20-25 minutes until peppers are tender and filling is cooked through.
7. Serve hot with a side salad.

Nutritional Data: 280 calories | 15g carbs | 20g protein | 15g fat | 3g fiber | 5g sugar

78. Lemon Thyme Chicken Drumsticks

⭐⭐⭐⭐⭐

🕐 **10 Minuten**   🍳🕐 **25 Minuten**   🍴 **4 servings**

INGREDIENTS

- 500g Chorizo, in Scheiben geschnitten
- 500g Kartoffeln, gewürfelt
- 1 rote Paprika, in Streifen geschnitten
- 1 Zwiebel, gewürfelt
- 2 Knoblauchzehen, fein gehackt
- 1 TL Paprikapulver
- Salz und frisch gemahlener schwarzer Pfeffer
- Frische Petersilie zur Garnierung

INSTRUCTIONS

1. In a bowl, mix together olive oil, lemon zest, lemon juice, minced garlic, chopped fresh thyme, salt, and pepper.
2. Add the chicken drumsticks to the marinade and let marinate for at least 15 minutes.
3. Preheat the air fryer to 375°F (190°C).
4. Place the marinated chicken drumsticks in the air fryer basket.
5. Air fry for 25-30 minutes, flipping halfway through, until chicken is golden and cooked through.
6. Serve hot with your favorite side dishes.

Nutritional Data: 320 calories | 0g carbs | 25g protein | 22g fat | 0g fiber | 0g sugar

79. Spicy Chorizo and Potato Pan

★ ★ ★ ★

🕐 **15 Minuten**   ♨🕐 **25 Minuten**   🍴 **4 servings**

INGREDIENTS

- 8 oz chorizo sausage, sliced
- 2 potatoes, diced
- 1 onion, sliced
- 1 red bell pepper, sliced
- 1 green bell pepper, sliced
- 2 cloves garlic, minced
- 2 tablespoons olive oil
- 1 teaspoon paprika
- Salt and pepper to taste

INSTRUCTIONS

1. Preheat the air fryer to 375°F (190°C).
2. In a bowl, toss together sliced chorizo sausage, diced potatoes, sliced onion, sliced red bell pepper, sliced green bell pepper, minced garlic, olive oil, paprika, salt, and pepper.
3. Transfer the mixture to the air fryer basket.
4. Air fry for 20-25 minutes, shaking the basket halfway through, until potatoes are tender and chorizo is crispy.
5. Serve hot as a main dish or with crusty bread.

Nutritional Data: 350 calories | 20g carbs | 15g protein | 25g fat | 4g fiber | 4g sugar

80. Beef Fillet with Herb Crust

★ ★ ★ ★ ★

🕐 **15 Minuten**   ♨🕐 **20 Minuten**   🍴 **2 servings**

INGREDIENTS

- 2 beef fillets (about 6 oz each)
- 2 tablespoons Dijon mustard
- 1/2 cup breadcrumbs
- 2 tablespoons chopped fresh parsley
- 2 tablespoons chopped fresh thyme
- 2 cloves garlic, minced
- 2 tablespoons olive oil
- Salt and pepper to taste

INSTRUCTIONS

1. Preheat the air fryer to 400°F (200°C).
2. Season the beef fillets with salt and pepper.
3. Brush each fillet with Dijon mustard.
4. In a bowl, mix together breadcrumbs, chopped fresh parsley, chopped fresh thyme, minced garlic, olive oil, salt, and pepper to form a crust.
5. Press the herb crust onto the mustard-coated side of each beef fillet.
6. Place the beef fillets in the air fryer basket.
7. Air fry for 18-20 minutes for medium-rare, adjusting the time based on desired doneness.
8. Let the beef fillets rest for a few minutes before serving.
9. Serve hot with roasted vegetables or a side salad.

Nutritional Data: 400 calories | 15g carbs | 25g protein | 28g fat | 2g fiber | 2g sugar

81. Classic Wiener Schnitzel

★★★★

🕐 **15 Minuten**   🍳🕐 **12 Minuten**   🍴 **2 servings**

INGREDIENTS

- 2 veal or pork cutlets
- 1/2 cup all-purpose flour
- 2 eggs, beaten
- 1 cup breadcrumbs
- Salt and pepper to taste
- Lemon wedges for serving

INSTRUCTIONS

1. Season the veal or pork cutlets with salt and pepper.
2. Set up three shallow dishes: one with flour, one with beaten eggs, and one with breadcrumbs.
3. Dredge each cutlet in the flour, then dip into the beaten eggs, and coat with breadcrumbs, pressing gently to adhere.
4. Preheat the air fryer to 375°F (190°C).
5. Place the breaded cutlets in the air fryer basket in a single layer.
6. Air fry for 6 minutes, then flip the cutlets and air fry for an additional 6 minutes until golden and crispy.
7. Serve hot with lemon wedges.

Nutritional Data: 420 calories | 30g carbs | 25g protein | 20g fat | 2g fiber | 1g sugar

82. Greek Minced Lamb Meatballs

★★★★★

🕐 **20 Minuten**   🍳🕐 **12 Minuten**   🍴 **4 servings**

INGREDIENTS

- 1 pound ground lamb
- 1/2 cup breadcrumbs
- 1/4 cup chopped fresh parsley
- 1/4 cup chopped fresh mint
- 1/4 cup crumbled feta cheese
- 1 egg, beaten
- 2 cloves garlic, minced
- 1 teaspoon dried oregano
- Salt and pepper to taste

INSTRUCTIONS

1. In a bowl, mix together ground lamb, breadcrumbs, chopped fresh parsley, chopped fresh mint, crumbled feta cheese, beaten egg, minced garlic, dried oregano, salt, and pepper.
2. Form the mixture into meatballs, about 1 inch in diameter.
3. Preheat the air fryer to 375°F (190°C).
4. Place the meatballs in the air fryer basket.
5. Air fry for 10-12 minutes, shaking the basket halfway through, until meatballs are cooked through and golden.
6. Serve hot with tzatziki sauce and pita bread.

Nutritional Data: 320 calories | 15g carbs | 20g protein | 20g fat | 2g fiber | 1g sugar

83. Pork Belly with Asian BBQ Glaze

★★★★☆

🕐 **14 Minuten**　　♨🕐 **45 Minuten**　　🍴 **2 servings**

INGREDIENTS

- 1 pound pork belly, skin removed and sliced
- 1/4 cup hoisin sauce
- 2 tablespoons soy sauce
- 1 tablespoon honey
- 1 tablespoon rice vinegar
- 2 cloves garlic, minced
- 1 teaspoon grated ginger
- Sesame seeds and chopped green onions for garnish

INSTRUCTIONS

1. In a bowl, mix together hoisin sauce, soy sauce, honey, rice vinegar, minced garlic, and grated ginger to make the Asian BBQ glaze.
2. Brush the pork belly slices with the glaze, ensuring they are evenly coated.
3. Marinate the pork belly slices in the glaze for at least 30 minutes.
4. Preheat the air fryer to 375°F (190°C).
5. Place the marinated pork belly slices in the air fryer basket.
6. Air fry for 40-45 minutes, flipping halfway through, until pork belly is crispy and caramelized.
7. Serve hot, garnished with sesame seeds and chopped green onions.

Nutritional Data: 450 calories | 10g carbs | 25g protein | 35g fat | 0g fiber | 8g sugar

84. Korean Chicken Wings

★★★★★

🕐 **20 Minuten**　　♨🕐 **25 Minuten**　　🍴 **4 servings**

INGREDIENTS

- 2 pounds chicken wings, separated into drumettes and flats
- 1/4 cup soy sauce
- 2 tablespoons gochujang (Korean chili paste)
- 2 tablespoons honey
- 2 cloves garlic, minced
- 1 teaspoon grated ginger
- 2 green onions, chopped for garnish
- Sesame seeds for garnish

INSTRUCTIONS

1. In a bowl, mix together soy sauce, gochujang, honey, minced garlic, and grated ginger to make the Korean marinade.
2. Place the chicken wings in a large resealable plastic bag and pour the marinade over them. Seal the bag and massage to coat the wings evenly. Marinate in the refrigerator for at least 1 hour or overnight.
3. Preheat the air fryer to 400°F (200°C).
4. Remove the chicken wings from the marinade and shake off any excess.
5. Place the chicken wings in the air fryer basket in a single layer, making sure they are not overcrowded.
6. Air fry for 22-25 minutes, flipping halfway through, until wings are cooked through and crispy.
7. Transfer the cooked wings to a serving platter and garnish with chopped green onions and sesame seeds.
8. Serve hot with a side of kimchi or pickled radish.

Nutritional Data: 350 calories | 10g carbs | 25g protein | 22g fat | 1g fiber | 8g sugar

85. Air Fryer Style Beef Goulash

★★★★

🕐 20 Minuten   ♨🕐 40 Minuten   🍴 4 servings

INGREDIENTS

- 1 pound beef stew meat, cubed
- 2 tablespoons all-purpose flour
- 2 tablespoons olive oil
- 1 onion, chopped
- 2 cloves garlic, minced
- 1 red bell pepper, chopped
- 1 green bell pepper, chopped
- 2 tablespoons tomato paste
- 1 cup beef broth
- 1 teaspoon paprika
- 1/2 teaspoon caraway seeds
- Salt and pepper to taste

INSTRUCTIONS

1. In a bowl, toss the beef stew meat with flour until evenly coated.
2. Preheat the air fryer to 375°F (190°C).
3. Heat olive oil in a skillet over medium heat. Add the coated beef cubes and cook until browned on all sides. Remove from the skillet and set aside.
4. In the same skillet, add chopped onion, minced garlic, red bell pepper, and green bell pepper. Cook until softened.
5. Stir in tomato paste, beef broth, paprika, caraway seeds, salt, and pepper. Cook for a few minutes until the sauce thickens.
6. Return the browned beef cubes to the skillet and stir to combine with the sauce.
7. Transfer the beef mixture to the air fryer basket.
8. Air fry for 25-30 minutes, stirring halfway through, until the beef is tender and the sauce is thickened.
9. Serve hot with mashed potatoes or crusty bread.

Nutritional Data: 320 calories | 15g carbs | 25g protein | 18g fat | 3g fiber | 5g sugar

86. Stuffed Chicken Breast with Spinach and Feta

★★★★★

🕐 20 Minuten   ♨🕐 25 Minuten   🍴 2 servings

INGREDIENTS

- 2 boneless, skinless chicken breasts
- 2 cups fresh spinach leaves
- 1/4 cup crumbled feta cheese
- 2 cloves garlic, minced
- 1 tablespoon olive oil
- Salt and pepper to taste

INSTRUCTIONS

1. Preheat the air fryer to 375°F (190°C).
2. Butterfly each chicken breast by slicing horizontally but not all the way through, then open like a book.
3. In a skillet, heat olive oil over medium heat. Add minced garlic and cook until fragrant.
4. Add fresh spinach leaves to the skillet and cook until wilted. Remove from heat.
5. Lay the chicken breasts flat and season with salt and pepper.
6. Spoon the cooked spinach mixture onto one half of each chicken breast, then sprinkle with crumbled feta cheese.
7. Fold the other half of the chicken breast over the filling to enclose it.
8. Secure the stuffed chicken breasts with toothpicks if needed.
9. Place the stuffed chicken breasts in the air fryer basket.
10. Air fry for 20-25 minutes until chicken is cooked through and golden.
11. Serve hot with your favorite side dishes.

Nutritional Data: 280 calories | 3g carbs | 30g protein | 15g fat | 2g fiber | 1g sugar

87. Italian Meatballs in Tomato Sauce

★★★★

🕐 **25 Minuten**   ♨🕐 **20 Minuten**   🍴 **4 servings**

INGREDIENTS

- 1 pound ground beef
- 1/2 cup breadcrumbs
- 1/4 cup grated Parmesan cheese
- 1 egg, beaten
- 2 cloves garlic, minced
- 1 tablespoon chopped fresh parsley
- Salt and pepper to taste For the sauce:
- 2 cups marinara sauce
- 1 teaspoon dried oregano
- 1/2 teaspoon dried basil
- 1/2 teaspoon red pepper flakes (optional)

INSTRUCTIONS

1. In a bowl, combine ground beef, breadcrumbs, grated Parmesan cheese, beaten egg, minced garlic, chopped fresh parsley, salt, and pepper. Mix until well combined.
2. Shape the mixture into meatballs, about 1 inch in diameter.
3. Preheat the air fryer to 375°F (190°C).
4. Place the meatballs in the air fryer basket in a single layer.
5. Air fry for 12-15 minutes, shaking the basket halfway through, until meatballs are browned and cooked through.
6. In a small saucepan, heat marinara sauce over medium heat. Stir in dried oregano, dried basil, and red pepper flakes (if using). Cook until heated through.
7. Serve the cooked meatballs with the warm marinara sauce.

Nutritional Data: 350 calories | 10g carbs | 25g protein | 22g fat | 2g fiber | 5g sugar

88. Pork Fillet with Apple Mustard Sauce

★★★★★

🕐 **15 Minuten**   ♨🕐 **25 Minuten**   🍴 **2 servings**

INGREDIENTS

- 1 pork fillet (tenderloin), about 1 pound
- 2 tablespoons olive oil
- 2 apples, peeled, cored, and sliced
- 1/4 cup apple cider vinegar
- 2 tablespoons Dijon mustard
- 2 tablespoons honey
- Salt and pepper to taste

INSTRUCTIONS

1. Season the pork fillet with salt and pepper.
2. Preheat the air fryer to 375°F (190°C).
3. Heat olive oil in a skillet over medium-high heat. Add the pork fillet and sear on all sides until golden brown.
4. Transfer the seared pork fillet to the air fryer basket.
5. Air fry for 20-25 minutes until pork is cooked through, flipping halfway through.
6. In the same skillet used to sear the pork, add sliced apples, apple cider vinegar, Dijon mustard, honey, salt, and pepper. Cook until the apples are soft and the sauce has thickened.
7. Slice the cooked pork fillet and serve with the apple mustard sauce.

Nutritional Data: 380 calories | 15g carbs | 30g protein | 20g fat | 2g fiber | 12g sugar

VEGAN

89. Crispy Tofu Nuggets with Sweet and Sour Sauce

★★★★★

🕐 15 Minuten   ♨🕐 20 Minuten   🍴 4 servings

INGREDIENTS

- 1 block (14 oz) firm tofu, pressed and drained
- 1/2 cup all-purpose flour
- 1/2 cup cornstarch
- 1 teaspoon garlic powder
- 1 teaspoon onion powder
- 1/2 teaspoon paprika
- Salt and pepper to taste
- Vegetable oil, for frying

INSTRUCTIONS

1. Marinate the tofu with soy sauce, garlic powder, paprika powder, salt and pepper.
2. Dip the tofu in the panko breadcrumbs so that all sides are covered.
3. Place the tofu croquettes in the air fryer and bake at 180 °C for about 20 minutes until crispy.

Serve with sweet and sour sauce.

Nutritional Data: 220 calories | 20g carbs | 10g protein | 8g fat | 8g fiber | 6g sugar

90. Crispy Chickpea Snacks with Paprika and Cumin

★★★★★

🕐 15 Minuten   ♨🕐 20 Minuten   🍴 4 servings

INGREDIENTS

- 2 cans (15 ounces each) chickpeas, drained and rinsed
- 2 tablespoons olive oil
- 1 teaspoon smoked paprika
- 1 teaspoon ground cumin
- 1/2 teaspoon garlic powder
- Salt to taste

INSTRUCTIONS

1. Preheat the air fryer to 400°F (200°C).
2. Pat dry the drained and rinsed chickpeas with a paper towel to remove excess moisture.
3. In a bowl, toss together chickpeas, olive oil, smoked paprika, ground cumin, garlic powder, and salt until chickpeas are evenly coated.
4. Spread the seasoned chickpeas in a single layer in the air fryer basket.
5. Air fry for 18-20 minutes, shaking the basket halfway through, until chickpeas are crispy and golden brown.
6. Let the chickpeas cool slightly before serving as a crunchy snack or topping for salads.

Nutritional Data: 220 calories | 30g carbs | 10g protein | 8g fat | 8g fiber | 3g sugar

91. Vegan Zucchini Fries with Garlic Aioli

⭐⭐⭐⭐⭐

🕐 **15 Minuten**   🍳🕐 **15 Minuten**   🍴 **4 servings**

INGREDIENTS

- 2 medium zucchini, cut into sticks
- 1 cup panko breadcrumbs
- 1/4 cup nutritional yeast
- 1 teaspoon garlic powder
- 1/2 teaspoon smoked paprika
- Salt and pepper to taste
- Cooking spray For the garlic aioli:
- 1/2 cup vegan mayonnaise
- 2 cloves garlic, minced
- 1 tablespoon lemon juice
- Salt and pepper to taste

INSTRUCTIONS

1. Preheat the air fryer to 375°F (190°C).
2. In a shallow dish, combine panko breadcrumbs, nutritional yeast, garlic powder, smoked paprika, salt, and pepper.
3. Dip zucchini sticks into the breadcrumb mixture, pressing gently to adhere.
4. Lightly coat the breaded zucchini sticks with cooking spray.
5. Arrange the coated zucchini sticks in a single layer in the air fryer basket.
6. Air fry for 12-15 minutes, flipping halfway through, until zucchini fries are crispy and golden brown.
7. While the zucchini fries are cooking, prepare the garlic aioli by mixing together vegan mayonnaise, minced garlic, lemon juice, salt, and pepper in a small bowl.
8. Serve the hot zucchini fries with the garlic aioli for dipping.

Nutritional Data : 120 calories | 20g carbs | 5g protein | 3g fat | 3g fiber | 4g sugar

---

92. Vegetable Tempura with Teriyaki Dip

⭐⭐⭐⭐

🕐 **20 Minuten**   🍳🕐 **15 Minuten**   🍴 **4 servings**

INGREDIENTS

- Assorted vegetables (such as bell peppers, broccoli florets, sweet potatoes, and zucchini), cut into bite-sized pieces
- 1 cup all-purpose flour
- 1 cup ice-cold water
- 1/2 teaspoon salt
- Cooking spray For the teriyaki dip:
- 1/4 cup soy sauce
- 2 tablespoons water
- 1 tablespoon rice vinegar
- 1 tablespoon brown sugar
- 1 teaspoon grated ginger
- 1 clove garlic, minced

INSTRUCTIONS

1. Preheat the air fryer to 375°F (190°C).
2. In a bowl, whisk together all-purpose flour, ice-cold water, and salt until just combined (it's okay if there are lumps).
3. Dip assorted vegetable pieces into the tempura batter, shaking off any excess.
4. Lightly coat the battered vegetables with cooking spray.
5. Arrange the coated vegetables in a single layer in the air fryer basket.
6. Air fry for 12-15 minutes, flipping halfway through, until tempura is crispy and golden brown.
7. While the vegetables are cooking, prepare the teriyaki dip by combining soy sauce, water, rice vinegar, brown sugar, grated ginger, and minced garlic in a small saucepan. Cook over medium heat until the sugar has dissolved and the mixture has slightly thickened. If desired, add the cornstarch-water mixture and cook until further thickened.
8. Serve the hot vegetable tempura with the teriyaki dip on the side.

Nutritional Data: 150 calories | 25g carbs | 3g protein | 4g fat | 2g fiber | 5g sugar

93. Moroccan Falafel Balls with Tahini Dressing

★★★★★

🕐 20 Minuten   🍳🕐 15 Minuten   🍴 4 servings

INGREDIENTS

- 1 can (15 ounces) chickpeas, drained and rinsed
- 1 small onion, chopped
- 2 cloves garlic, minced
- 1/4 cup chopped fresh parsley
- 1/4 cup chopped fresh cilantro
- 1 teaspoon ground cumin
- 1 teaspoon ground coriander
- 1/2 teaspoon smoked paprika
- 1/4 teaspoon cayenne pepper
- Salt and pepper to taste
- 2 tablespoons all-purpose flour
- 1 teaspoon baking powder
- Vegetable oil for frying For the tahini dressing:
- 1/4 cup tahini
- 2 tablespoons lemon juice
- 2 tablespoons water
- 1 clove garlic, minced

INSTRUCTIONS

1. In a food processor, combine chickpeas, chopped onion, minced garlic, chopped parsley, chopped cilantro, ground cumin, ground coriander, smoked paprika, cayenne pepper, salt, and pepper. Pulse until the mixture is coarsely ground but not pureed.
2. Transfer the chickpea mixture to a bowl and stir in all-purpose flour and baking powder until well combined.
3. Shape the mixture into small balls and place them on a baking sheet lined with parchment paper.
4. Preheat the air fryer to 375°F (190°C).
5. Lightly coat the falafel balls with vegetable oil.
6. Arrange the falafel balls in a single layer in the air fryer basket.
7. Air fry for 12-15 minutes, shaking the basket halfway through, until falafel balls are crispy and golden brown.
8. While the falafel balls are cooking, prepare the tahini dressing by whisking together tahini, lemon juice, water, minced garlic, and salt in a small bowl until smooth.

Nutritional Data : 180 calories | 20g carbs | 6g protein | 8g fat | 5g fiber | 2g sugar

94. Potato and Carrot Rösti

★★★★

🕐 20 Minuten   🍳🕐 15 Minuten   🍴 4 servings

INGREDIENTS

- 2 large potatoes, peeled and grated
- 2 large carrots, peeled and grated
- 1 small onion, grated
- 2 tablespoons all-purpose flour
- 1 teaspoon salt
- 1/2 teaspoon black pepper
- 2 tablespoons vegetable oil

INSTRUCTIONS

1. In a large bowl, combine grated potatoes, grated carrots, grated onion, all-purpose flour, salt, and black pepper. Mix until well combined.
2. Preheat the air fryer to 375°F (190°C).
3. Divide the potato-carrot mixture into equal portions and shape each portion into a round patty.
4. Brush both sides of the patties with vegetable oil.
5. Arrange the patties in a single layer in the air fryer basket.
6. Air fry for 18-20 minutes, flipping halfway through, until the rösti patties are crispy and golden brown.
7. Serve hot as a side dish or breakfast item with sour cream or applesauce on the side.

Nutritional Data: 160 calories | 20g carbs | 2g protein | 8g fat | 3g fiber | 3g sugar

95. Baked Avocado Wedges with Salsa Verde

★★★★★

🕐 15 Minuten   ♨🕐 10 Minuten   🍴 4 servings

INSTRUCTIONS

1. Preheat the air fryer to 375°F (190°C).
2. Set up a breading station with three shallow dishes: one with all-purpose flour, one with beaten eggs, and one with breadcrumbs mixed with smoked paprika, garlic powder, salt, and pepper.
3. Dredge avocado wedges in flour, then dip them in beaten eggs, and finally coat them in breadcrumb mixture, pressing gently to adhere.
4. Place the breaded avocado wedges on a baking sheet lined with parchment paper.
5. Lightly coat the avocado wedges with cooking spray.
6. Arrange the avocado wedges in a single layer in the air fryer basket.
7. Air fry for 12-15 minutes, flipping halfway through, until the avocado wedges are crispy and golden brown.
8. While the avocado wedges are cooking, prepare the salsa verde by blending together cilantro leaves, parsley leaves, garlic cloves, chopped green onions, chopped jalapeño pepper, lime juice, olive oil, salt, and pepper until smooth.
9. Serve the hot baked avocado wedges with salsa verde on the side for dipping.

INGREDIENTS

- 2 ripe avocados, pitted and sliced into wedges
- 1/2 cup all-purpose flour
- 2 eggs, beaten
- 1 cup breadcrumbs
- 1 teaspoon smoked paprika
- 1/2 teaspoon garlic powder
- Salt and pepper to taste

Nutritional Data : 200 calories | 20g carbs | 4g protein | 12g fat | 8g fiber | 2g sugar

96 Vegan Pizza Rolls with Cashew Cheese

★★★★

🕐 25 Minuten   ♨🕐 15 Minuten   🍴 4 servings

INSTRUCTIONS

1. Roll out the pizza dough and spread with the tomato puree. Top with oregano, basil, cashew cheese and vegetables.
2. Roll up the dough and cut into slices.
3. Place the pizza rolls in the air fryer and bake at 180°C for approx. 15 minutes until golden brown.
4. Serve warm.

INGREDIENTS

- 1 1/2 cups all-purpose flour
- 1 teaspoon active dry yeast
- 1/2 teaspoon salt
- 1/2 teaspoon sugar
- 1/2 cup warm water
- 1 tablespoon olive oil For the cashew cheese:
- 1 cup raw cashews, soaked in water for 4 hours or overnight, drained
- 2 tablespoons nutritional yeast
- 1 tablespoon lemon juice
- 1 clove garlic, minced
- Salt and pepper to taste

Nutritional Data : 320 calories | 45g carbs | 8g protein | 12g fat | 4g fiber | 2g sugar

97. Sweet Potato and Black Bean Burritos

★★★★★

🕐 **30 Minuten** 🍳🕐 **20 Minuten** 🍴 **4 servings**

INGREDIENTS

- 2 medium sweet potatoes, peeled and diced
- 1 can (15 ounces) black beans, drained and rinsed
- 1 small red onion, diced
- 1 bell pepper, diced
- 2 cloves garlic, minced
- 1 teaspoon ground cumin
- 1 teaspoon chili powder
- Salt and pepper to taste
- 4 large flour tortillas
- 1 cup shredded cheddar cheese (optional)
- Salsa, guacamole, and sour cream for serving

INSTRUCTIONS

1. Mix the sweet potatoes, black beans, paprika, onion and cumin in a bowl. Season with salt and pepper.
2. Fill the tortillas with the mixture and roll into burritos.
3. Place the burritos in the air fryer and bake at 180°C for approx. 20 minutes until crispy.
4. Serve with vegan sour cream.

Nutritional Data : 350 calories | 55g carbs | 12g protein | 8g fat | 8g fiber | 5g sugar

98. Ratatouille Vegetable Chips with Herbs de Provence

★★★★

🕐 **15 Minuten** 🍳🕐 **20 Minuten** 🍴 **4 servings**

INGREDIENTS

- 1 medium eggplant, thinly sliced
- 2 small zucchinis, thinly sliced
- 2 small yellow squash, thinly sliced
- 2 medium tomatoes, thinly sliced
- 2 tablespoons olive oil
- 1 tablespoon Herbs de Provence
- Salt and pepper to taste

INSTRUCTIONS

1. Preheat the air fryer to 375°F (190°C).
2. Arrange the thinly sliced vegetables in a single layer in the air fryer basket.
3. Drizzle olive oil over the vegetables and sprinkle Herbs de Provence, salt, and pepper evenly.
4. Air fry for 20-25 minutes, flipping halfway through, until the vegetables are crispy and golden brown.
5. Serve hot as a side dish or snack.

Nutritional Data: 120 calories | 10g carbs | 2g protein | 9g fat | 4g fiber | 5g sugar

DESSERTS

99. Apple Cinnamon Rings with Vanilla Sauce

★★★★★

🕐 15 Minuten   ♨🕐 10 Minuten   🍴 4 servings

INGREDIENTS

- 2 large apples, cored and thinly sliced into rings
- 1/2 cup all-purpose flour
- 1 teaspoon ground cinnamon
- 1/4 teaspoon ground nutmeg
- 1/4 teaspoon ground cloves
- 1/4 teaspoon salt
- 1/2 cup milk
- 1 cup breadcrumbs
- Cooking spray

INSTRUCTIONS

1. In a shallow dish, combine all-purpose flour, ground cinnamon, ground nutmeg, ground cloves, and salt. In another shallow dish, pour milk.
2. Dip apple slices into the flour mixture, then dip into milk, and finally coat with breadcrumbs.
3. Preheat the air fryer to 375°F (190°C).
4. Lightly coat the coated apple slices with cooking spray.
5. Arrange the apple slices in a single layer in the air fryer basket.
6. Air fry for 8-10 minutes, flipping halfway through, until the apple rings are golden brown and crispy.
7. Meanwhile, prepare the vanilla sauce by whisking together milk and cornstarch in a saucepan over medium heat until thickened. Stir in maple syrup and vanilla extract.
8. Serve the hot apple cinnamon rings with warm vanilla sauce drizzled on top.

Nutritional Data : 160 calories | 30g carbs | 2g protein | 4g fat | 4g fiber | 12g sugar

100. Banana Bread with Chocolate Chips

★★★★

🕐 15 Minuten   ♨🕐 20Minuten   🍴 4 servings

INGREDIENTS

- 2 ripe bananas, mashed
- 1/3 cup melted butter
- 1/2 cup granulated sugar
- 1 egg, beaten
- 1 teaspoon vanilla extract
- 1 1/2 cups all-purpose flour
- 1 teaspoon baking powder
- 1/2 teaspoon baking soda
- 1/4 teaspoon salt
- 1/2 cup chocolate chips

INSTRUCTIONS

1. Preheat the air fryer to 320°F (160°C).
2. In a mixing bowl, combine mashed bananas, melted butter, granulated sugar, beaten egg, and vanilla extract. Mix until well combined.
3. In another bowl, sift together all-purpose flour, baking powder, baking soda, and salt.
4. Gradually add the dry ingredients to the wet ingredients, stirring until just combined.
5. Fold in chocolate chips.
6. Lightly grease a loaf pan that fits into your air fryer.
7. Pour the batter into the loaf pan and spread it evenly.
8. Place the loaf pan in the air fryer basket.
9. Air fry for 45-50 minutes or until a toothpick inserted into the center comes out clean.
10. Remove the banana bread from the air fryer and let it cool in the pan for 10 minutes before transferring it to a wire rack to cool completely.

Nutritional Data: 240 calories | 36g carbs | 3g protein | 10g fat | 2g fiber | 20g sugar

101. Vegan Blueberry Muffins

★★★★★

🕐 20 Minuten   ♨🕐 10 Minuten   🍴 8 servings

INGREDIENTS

- 2 cups all-purpose flour
- 1/2 cup granulated sugar
- 1 tablespoon baking powder
- 1/4 teaspoon salt
- 1 cup almond milk (or any plant-based milk)
- 1/4 cup vegetable oil
- 1 teaspoon vanilla extract
- 1 cup fresh or frozen blueberries

INSTRUCTIONS

1. Preheat the air fryer to 320°F (160°C).
2. In a mixing bowl, whisk together all-purpose flour, granulated sugar, baking powder, and salt.
3. In another bowl, combine almond milk, vegetable oil, and vanilla extract.
4. Gradually add the wet ingredients to the dry ingredients, stirring until just combined.
5. Gently fold in the blueberries.
6. Line a muffin tin with paper liners or lightly grease the muffin cups.
7. Divide the batter evenly among the muffin cups, filling each about 2/3 full.
8. Place the muffin tin in the air fryer basket.
9. Air fry for 20-25 minutes or until a toothpick inserted into the center of a muffin comes out clean.
10. Remove the muffins from the air fryer and let them cool in the tin for 5 minutes before transferring them to a wire rack to cool completely.

Nutritional Data: 160 calories | 24g carbs | 2g protein | 7g fat | 1g fiber | 10g sugar

102. Baked Cinnamon Rolls

★★★★★

🕐 30 Minuten   ♨🕐 15 Minuten   🍴 6 servings

INGREDIENTS

- For the dough:
- 1 package (2 1/4 teaspoons) active dry yeast
- 1 cup warm milk (110°F/45°C)
- 1/2 cup granulated sugar
- 1/3 cup unsalted butter, melted
- 2 large eggs
- 4 cups all-purpose flour
- 1 teaspoon salt For the filling:
- 1/2 cup unsalted butter, softened
- 1 cup packed brown sugar
- 2 tablespoons ground cinnamon For the icing:
- 1 cup powdered sugar
- 2 tablespoons milk
- 1/2 teaspoon vanilla extract

INSTRUCTIONS

1. In a small bowl, dissolve yeast in warm milk and let it sit for about 5 minutes until frothy.
2. In a large mixing bowl, combine the yeast mixture with granulated sugar, melted unsalted butter, and eggs.
3. Gradually add flour and salt to the wet ingredients, mixing until a dough forms.
4. Knead the dough on a floured surface until it becomes smooth and elastic, about 5 minutes.
5. Place the dough in a greased bowl, cover with a clean kitchen towel, and let it rise in a warm place for about 1 hour or until doubled in size.
6. Once the dough has risen, punch it down and roll it out on a floured surface into a large rectangle, about 1/4 inch thick.
7. Spread softened unsalted butter evenly over the dough.
8. In a small bowl, mix together packed brown sugar and ground cinnamon, then sprinkle the mixture over the buttered dough.
9. Starting from one long side, roll up the dough tightly into a log.
10. Cut the log into 12 equal slices and place them in a greased baking dish.
11. Cover the dish with a clean kitchen towel and let the rolls rise for another 30 minutes.
12. Preheat the air fryer to 350°F (180°C).
13. Place the baking dish in the air fryer basket and bake the cinnamon rolls for 12-15 minutes or until golden brown.
14. While the rolls are baking, prepare the icing by whisking together powdered sugar, milk, and vanilla extract until smooth.
15. Once the rolls are done, remove them from the air fryer and drizzle the icing over the warm rolls.
16. Serve the cinnamon rolls warm and enjoy!

Nutritional Data: 300 calories | 45g carbs | 5g protein | 12g fat | 2g fiber | 25g sugar

103. Chocolate Lava Cake

★★★★★

🕐 20 Minuten ♨🕐 8 Minuten 🍴 4 servings

INGREDIENTS

- 4 ounces dark chocolate
- 1/2 cup unsalted butter
- 1/4 cup granulated sugar
- 2 large eggs
- 2 large egg yolks
- 1/2 teaspoon vanilla extract
- 1/4 cup all-purpose flour
- Pinch of salt
- Powdered sugar, for dusting

INSTRUCTIONS

1. Preheat the air fryer to 375°F (190°C).
2. In a microwave-safe bowl, melt dark chocolate and unsalted butter together in short bursts, stirring until smooth.
3. In a separate bowl, whisk together granulated sugar, eggs, egg yolks, and vanilla extract until well combined.
4. Gradually pour the melted chocolate mixture into the egg mixture, whisking constantly.
5. Sift in all-purpose flour and a pinch of salt, and fold gently until just combined.
6. Grease four ramekins and divide the batter equally among them.
7. Place the ramekins in the air fryer basket.
8. Air fry for 8 minutes, or until the edges are set but the center is still slightly jiggly.
9. Carefully remove the ramekins from the air fryer and let them cool for a minute.
10. Dust with powdered sugar and serve immediately, optionally with fresh berries on the side.

Nutritional Data: 320 calories | 25g carbs | 5g protein | 23g fat | 2g fiber | 20g sugar

104. Plum Crumble with Oatmeal Streusel

★★★★☆

🕐 15 Minuten ♨🕐 20 Minuten 🍴 4 servings

INSTRUCTIONS

1. Preheat the air fryer to 375°F (190°C).
2. In a mixing bowl, toss sliced plums with granulated sugar, cornstarch, ground cinnamon, and vanilla extract until evenly coated.
3. In another bowl, combine old-fashioned oats, all-purpose flour, brown sugar, ground cinnamon, and a pinch of salt. Mix well.
4. Add chilled and cubed unsalted butter to the oat mixture. Use your fingertips to rub the butter into the dry ingredients until the mixture resembles coarse crumbs.
5. Place the plum mixture into a baking dish that fits into your air fryer.
6. Sprinkle the oatmeal streusel evenly over the plum mixture.
7. Place the baking dish in the air fryer basket.
8. Air fry for 30-35 minutes, or until the plum filling is bubbling, and the streusel is golden brown and crisp.
9. Remove from the air fryer and let it cool slightly before serving.
10. Serve warm, optionally with a scoop of vanilla ice cream or a dollop of whipped cream.

INGREDIENTS

- 6 ripe plums, pitted and sliced
- 2 tablespoons granulated sugar
- 1 tablespoon cornstarch
- 1 teaspoon ground cinnamon
- 1/2 teaspoon vanilla extract For the oatmeal streusel
- 1/2 cup old-fashioned oats
- 1/4 cup all-purpose flour
- 1/4 cup brown sugar
- 1/4 teaspoon ground cinnamon
- Pinch of salt
- 3 tablespoons unsalted butter, chilled and cubed

Nutritional Data: 200 calories | 30g carbs | 2g protein | 8g fat | 3g fiber | 20g sugar

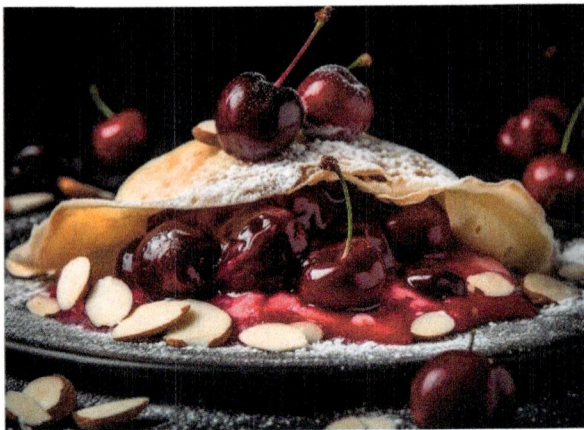

105.Kirsch-Clafoutis

★★★★★

🕐 10 Minuten   🍳🕐 30 Minuten   🍴 4 servings

INGREDIENTS

- 2 cups pitted cherries
- 3 eggs
- 1/2 cup granulated sugar
- 1 cup milk
- 1/2 cup all-purpose flour
- 1 teaspoon vanilla extract
- 1 tablespoon kirsch (cherry brandy), optional
- Powdered sugar, for dusting

INSTRUCTIONS

1. Preheat the air fryer to 350°F (180°C).
2. Grease a baking dish that fits into your air fryer.
3. Arrange pitted cherries in a single layer in the bottom of the baking dish.
4. In a mixing bowl, whisk together eggs and granulated sugar until pale and frothy.
5. Gradually whisk in milk, all-purpose flour, vanilla extract, and kirsch until smooth.
6. Pour the batter over the cherries in the baking dish.
7. Place the baking dish in the air fryer basket.
8. Air fry for 25-30 minutes, or until the clafoutis is set and golden brown on top.
9. Remove from the air fryer and let it cool slightly before serving.
10. Dust with powdered sugar and serve warm.

Nutritional Data: 250 calories | 35g carbs | 6g protein | 8g fat | 2g fiber | 20g sugar

106.Baked Pineapple Rings with Coconut Crust

★★★★

🕐 10 Minuten   🍳🕐 12 Minuten   🍴 4 servings

INGREDIENTS

- 1 ripe pineapple, peeled and cored
- 1/2 cup shredded coconut
- 2 tablespoons honey
- 1/4 teaspoon ground cinnamon
- Pinch of salt

INSTRUCTIONS

1. Preheat the air fryer to 375°F (190°C).
2. Slice the pineapple into rings.
3. In a shallow dish, combine shredded coconut, honey, ground cinnamon, and a pinch of salt.
4. Dip each pineapple ring into the coconut mixture, ensuring it's evenly coated on both sides.
5. Place the coated pineapple rings in a single layer in the air fryer basket.
6. Air fry for 12-15 minutes, flipping halfway through, until the coconut crust is golden brown and crispy.
7. Remove from the air fryer and let them cool slightly before serving.
8. Serve warm as a snack or dessert.

Nutritional Data: 150 calories | 35g carbs | 1g protein | 3g fat | 3g fiber | 25g sugar

107. Sweet Potato Brownies

★★★★★

🕐 20 Minuten   ♨🕐 30 Minuten   🍴 8 servings

INSTRUCTIONS

1. Preheat the air fryer to 350°F (180°C).
2. In a large mixing bowl, combine grated sweet potatoes, almond flour, cocoa powder, maple syrup, almond butter, melted coconut oil, vanilla extract, baking powder, and a pinch of salt. Mix well until thoroughly combined.
3. If using, fold in chocolate chips.
4. Grease a baking dish that fits into your air fryer.
5. Spread the sweet potato brownie batter evenly into the baking dish.
6. Place the baking dish in the air fryer basket.
7. Air fry for 20-25 minutes, or until the brownies are set and a toothpick inserted into the center comes out clean.
8. Remove from the air fryer and let them cool completely before slicing into squares.
9. Serve at room temperature and enjoy!

INGREDIENTS

- 2 medium sweet potatoes, peeled and grated
- 1/2 cup almond flour
- 1/4 cup cocoa powder
- 1/4 cup maple syrup
- 1/4 cup almond butter
- 2 tablespoons coconut oil, melted
- 1 teaspoon vanilla extract
- 1/2 teaspoon baking powder
- Pinch of salt

Nutritional Data: 200 calories | 25g carbs | 3g protein | 10g fat | 4g fiber | 10g sugar

108. Mini Apple Strudel

★★★★

🕐 25 Minuten   ♨🕐 15 Minuten   🍴 4 servings

INSTRUCTIONS

1. Preheat the air fryer to 375°F (190°C).
2. In a bowl, toss together apple slices, granulated sugar, ground cinnamon, raisins (if using), and lemon juice until well combined.
3. Place one sheet of phyllo pastry on a clean surface and brush it lightly with melted butter.
4. Repeat the process with the remaining sheets, layering them on top of each other and brushing each layer with butter.
5. Cut the layered phyllo pastry into 4 equal rectangles.
6. Place a spoonful of the apple mixture on one end of each rectangle.
7. Fold in the sides and roll up the phyllo pastry to enclose the filling, forming mini strudels.
8. Place the mini strudels seam side down in the air fryer basket.
9. Air fry for 12-15 minutes, or until the strudels are golden brown and crispy.
10. Remove from the air fryer and let them cool slightly before dusting with powdered sugar.
11. Serve warm and enjoy!

INGREDIENTS

- 2 medium apples, peeled, cored, and thinly sliced
- 1/4 cup granulated sugar
- 1 teaspoon ground cinnamon
- 1/4 cup raisins (optional)
- 1 tablespoon lemon juice
- 6 sheets phyllo pastry
- 4 tablespoons unsalted butter, melted
- Powdered sugar, for dusting

Nutritional Data: 150 calories | 20g carbs | 1g protein | 8g fat | 2g fiber | 10g sugar

109. Pear Tart Tatin

★★★★

🕐 20 Minuten   🍳🕐 25 Minuten   🍴 6 servings

INGREDIENTS

- 4 ripe pears, peeled, cored, and halved
- 1/4 cup unsalted butter
- 1/2 cup granulated sugar
- 1 teaspoon ground cinnamon
- 1 sheet puff pastry, thawed

INSTRUCTIONS

1. Melt the sugar in a pan until it caramelizes. Add the butter and vanilla extract.
2. Pour the caramel into a dish suitable for the air fryer, place the pear halves on top.
3. Place the puff pastry over the pears and press in the edges.
4. Bake at 180°C for approx. 25 minutes until the pastry is golden brown.
5. Turn out carefully and serve warm.

Nutritional Data: 250 calories | 30g carbs | 1g protein | 14g fat | 2g fiber | 20g sugar

110. Mandel-Croissants

★★★★★

🕐 15 Minuten   🍳🕐 15 Minuten   🍴 8 servings

INGREDIENTS

- 1 sheet puff pastry, thawed
- 1/2 cup almond paste
- 1 egg, beaten
- Sliced almonds, for garnish
- Powdered sugar, for dusting

INSTRUCTIONS

1. Mix the almonds, sugar, egg and milk into a paste.
2. Cut open the croissants and fill with the almond paste.
3. Bake at 180°C for approx. 10 minutes until risen and golden brown.
4. Dust with powdered sugar and serve.

Nutritional Data: 200 calories | 20g carbs | 5g protein | 12g fat | 2g fiber | 10g sugar

111. Strawberry Rhubarb Crumble

★★★★

🕐 15 Minuten | 🍳🕐 18 Minuten | 🍴 4 servings

INGREDIENTS

- 2 cups sliced strawberries
- 2 cups diced rhubarb
- 1/4 cup granulated sugar
- 1 tablespoon cornstarch
- 1 tablespoon lemon juice

INSTRUCTIONS

1. Place the strawberries and rhubarb in a bowl and mix with a little sugar.
2. For the crumble, mix the rolled oats, remaining sugar, butter and cinnamon into a crumbly mixture.
3. Place the fruit mixture in the air fryer, spread the crumble on top and bake at 180°C for approx. 18 minutes.
4. Serve warm, ideally with vanilla ice cream or whipped cream.

Nutritional Data: 250 calories | 35g carbs | 3g protein | 10g fat | 4g fiber | 20g sugar

112. Coconut Mango Roll

★★★★★

🕐 20 Minuten | 🍳🕐 12 Minuten | 🍴 6 servings

INSTRUCTIONS

1. Preheat the air fryer to 350°F (180°C).
2. In a mixing bowl, beat eggs and granulated sugar until pale and fluffy.
3. In another bowl, sift together all-purpose flour, cornstarch, baking powder, and a pinch of salt.
4. Gradually fold the dry ingredients into the egg mixture until just combined.
5. Line a baking tray with parchment paper and pour the batter onto it, spreading it evenly.
6. Air fry for 15-20 minutes, or until the sponge cake is cooked through and lightly golden.
7. Remove the sponge cake from the air fryer and let it cool completely.
8. In a bowl, mix together mango pulp, whipped cream, shredded coconut, and powdered sugar until well combined.
9. Spread the mango mixture evenly over the cooled sponge cake.
10. Carefully roll up the cake from one end to the other, forming a log.
11. Wrap the roll tightly in plastic wrap and refrigerate for at least 2 hours to set.
12. Slice the chilled roll into rounds before serving.

INGREDIENTS

- 4 large eggs
- 1/2 cup granulated sugar
- 1/2 cup all-purpose flour
- 1/4 cup cornstarch
- 1 teaspoon baking powder
- 1 cup mango pulp
- 1 cup whipped cream
- 1/2 cup shredded coconut
- 2 tablespoons powdered sugar

Nutritional Data: 220 calories | 30g carbs | 4g protein | 9g fat | 2g fiber | 20g sugar

113. Baked Lemon Ricotta Tarts

★★★★

🕐 **25 Minuten** 🍳🕐 **20 Minuten** 🍴 **6 servings**

INGREDIENTS

- For the tart crust:
- 1 1/2 cups all-purpose flour
- 1/2 cup unsalted butter, chilled and cubed
- 1/4 cup granulated sugar
- 1 large egg
- 1 tablespoon cold water
- Pinch of salt For the lemon ricotta filling:
- 1 cup ricotta cheese
- 1/4 cup granulated sugar
- Zest of 1 lemon
- 2 tablespoons lemon juice
- 1 large egg
- 1 tablespoon all-purpose flour
- Powdered sugar, for dusting

INSTRUCTIONS

1. Preheat the air fryer to 375°F (190°C).
2. In a food processor, combine all-purpose flour, chilled and cubed unsalted butter, granulated sugar, egg, cold water, and a pinch of salt. Pulse until the mixture resembles coarse crumbs.
3. Press the dough into individual tart pans, covering the bottom and sides evenly.
4. In a mixing bowl, whisk together ricotta cheese, granulated sugar, lemon zest, lemon juice, egg, and all-purpose flour until smooth.
5. Pour the lemon ricotta mixture into the prepared tart crusts.
6. Place the tart pans in the air fryer basket.
7. Air fry for 18-20 minutes, or until the tarts are set and the crust is golden brown.
8. Remove from the air fryer and let them cool slightly before dusting with powdered sugar.
9. Serve warm or at room temperature.

Nutritional Data: 280 calories | 30g carbs | 7g protein | 15g fat | 1g fiber | 15g sugar

114. Chocolate Chip Cookies

★★★★★

🕐 **15 Minuten** 🍳🕐 **10 Minuten** 🍴 **24 servings**

INGREDIENTS

- 1 cup unsalted butter, softened
- 3/4 cup granulated sugar
- 3/4 cup packed brown sugar
- 2 large eggs
- 1 teaspoon vanilla extract
- 2 1/4 cups all-purpose flour
- 1 teaspoon baking soda
- 1/2 teaspoon salt
- 2 cups semisweet chocolate chips

INSTRUCTIONS

1. Preheat the air fryer to 350°F (180°C).
2. In a large mixing bowl, cream together softened unsalted butter, granulated sugar, and packed brown sugar until light and fluffy.
3. Beat in eggs, one at a time, until well combined. Stir in vanilla extract.
4. In a separate bowl, whisk together all-purpose flour, baking soda, and salt.
5. Gradually add the dry ingredients to the wet ingredients, mixing until just combined.
6. Fold in semisweet chocolate chips until evenly distributed throughout the dough.
7. Drop rounded tablespoons of dough onto a parchment-lined baking tray, spacing them about 2 inches apart.
8. Place the baking tray in the air fryer basket.
9. Air fry for 8-10 minutes, or until the cookies are golden brown around the edges.
10. Remove from the air fryer and let them cool on the baking tray for a few minutes before transferring to a wire rack to cool completely.
11. Repeat with the remaining dough, if necessary.
12. Serve the cookies warm or at room temperature, and enjoy!

Nutritional Data: 180 calories | 20g carbs | 2g protein | 10g fat | 1g fiber | 15g sugar

115. Chocolate Banana Spring Rolls

★★★★

🕐 **20 Minuten** ♨🕐 **10 Minuten** 🍴 **6 servings**

INGREDIENTS

- 4 ripe bananas, peeled and halved lengthwise
- 8 egg roll wrappers
- 1/2 cup chocolate chips
- 1/4 cup unsalted butter, melted
- Powdered sugar, for dusting

INSTRUCTIONS

1. Preheat the air fryer to 375°F (190°C).
2. Place a halved banana and a few chocolate chips in the center of each egg roll wrapper.
3. Fold the sides of the wrapper over the banana and chocolate chips, then roll up tightly.
4. Brush each spring roll with melted unsalted butter.
5. Place the spring rolls in the air fryer basket in a single layer.
6. Air fry for 8-10 minutes, or until the spring rolls are golden brown and crispy.
7. Remove from the air fryer and let them cool slightly before dusting with powdered sugar.
8. Serve warm and enjoy as a delicious dessert or snack!

Nutritional Data: 250 calories | 35g carbs | 5g protein | 10g fat | 2g fiber | 20g sugar

116. Blueberry Cream Cheese Danish

★★★★★

🕐 **20 Minuten** ♨🕐 **15 Minuten** 🍴 **6 servings**

INGREDIENTS

- 1 sheet puff pastry, thawed
- 4 oz cream cheese, softened
- 1/4 cup granulated sugar
- 1 teaspoon vanilla extract
- 1 cup fresh blueberries
- 1 egg, beaten
- Powdered sugar, for dusting

INSTRUCTIONS

1. Preheat the air fryer to 375°F (190°C).
2. Roll out the puff pastry sheet on a lightly floured surface into a large rectangle. Cut into 8 equal squares.
3. In a mixing bowl, beat together softened cream cheese, granulated sugar, and vanilla extract until smooth.
4. Place a dollop of the cream cheese mixture in the center of each puff pastry square and spread it slightly.
5. Top each square with a handful of fresh blueberries.
6. Fold the corners of each square over the filling, leaving the center exposed.
7. Brush the edges of the pastry with beaten egg.
8. Place the danishes on a parchment-lined air fryer basket.
9. Air fry for 12-15 minutes, or until the pastries are puffed and golden brown.
10. Remove from the air fryer and let them cool slightly before dusting with powdered sugar.
11. Serve warm and enjoy!

Nutritional Data: 220 calories | 25g carbs | 4g protein | 12g fat | 1g fiber | 10g sugar

Exclusive bonus:

Extra video recipes with step-by-step explanations

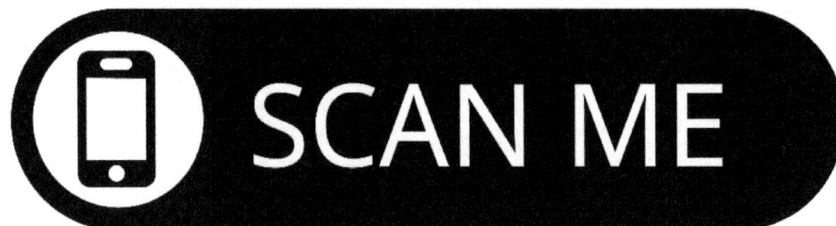

Printed in Great Britain
by Amazon